This Southern Metropolis

This Southern Metropolis
Life in Antebellum Mobile

MIKE BUNN

NEWSOUTH BOOKS
an imprint of
The University of Georgia Press
Athens

NSB

Published by NewSouth Books,
an imprint of the University of Georgia Press
Athens, Georgia 30602
https://ugapress.org/imprints/newsouth-books/

© 2024 by the University of Georgia Press
All rights reserved

Most NewSouth/University of Georgia Press titles are
available from popular e-book vendors.

Printed digitally

Library of Congress Cataloging-in-Publication Data
Names: Bunn, Mike, author.
Title: This southern metropolis : life in antebellum Mobile / Mike Bunn.
Other titles: Life in antebellum Mobile
Description: Athens, Georgia : NewSouth Books, an imprint of The University of Georgia Press, [2024] | Includes bibliographical references and index.
Identifiers: LCCN 2024009805 | ISBN 9781588385239 (hardback) | ISBN 9781588385246 (paperback) | ISBN 9781588385253 (epub) | ISBN 9781588385260 (pdf)
Subjects: LCSH: Travel writing—Alabama—Mobile. | Slavery—Alabama—Mobile—History—19th century. | Mobile (Ala.)—History—19th century. | Mobile (Ala.)—History—Anecdotes. | Mobile (Ala.)—Description and travel—Sources.
Classification: LCC F334.M6 B86 2023 | DDC 976.1/2209034—dc23/eng/20240313
LC record available at https://lccn.loc.gov/2024009805

For Drs. Edward and Dixie Hicks, who showed me the way

CONTENTS

ACKNOWLEDGMENTS IX

INTRODUCTION 1

CHAPTER 1
Getting There 8

CHAPTER 2
Arrival 21

CHAPTER 3
The Setting 34

CHAPTER 4
A Place for Business 55

CHAPTER 5
Dangers 69

CHAPTER 6
People and Lifestyles 81

CHAPTER 7
Slavery and the Enslaved 99

CHAPTER 8
Entertainment and Celebrations 118

AFTERWORD 131

NOTES 139

BIBLIOGRAPHY 153

INDEX 159

ACKNOWLEDGMENTS

The production of a book is always a team effort. In the research, editing, and arrangement of this volume, I have enjoyed the kind assistance of many individuals and institutions, and several are worthy of special notice. The staffs of a number of regional libraries have, as always, been consistently helpful. These include the Marx Library at the University of South Alabama, the Mobile Public Library, Daphne Public Library, Fairhope Public Library, and Southern History Department of the Birmingham Public Library. Bob Peck, a longtime volunteer with the Historic Mobile Preservation Society's Minnie Mitchell Archives, and Charles Torrey, research historian at the History Museum of Mobile, were especially kind and generous with their time. The multiple authors who have written about Mobile's history over the years, and whose work provides context for what I present, were, as a group, invaluable. If you have any interest in the history of this remarkable city, you should know the names Michael V. R. Thomason, Harriet Amos Doss, Elizabeth Barrett Gould, and John Sledge. I likewise owe a special debt of gratitude to the travelers who took the time to write about antebellum Mobile; this book is based on their words. By any measure, they rank among a distinct minority of visitors to the city during a foundational era, but without their work our understanding of that interlude in the community's history would be much less rich. Special thanks also are due the peer reviewers who took their valuable time to offer their thoughts on the original draft of the manuscript of this book and how it might be improved, and to the production team at the University of Georgia Press, which assisted me in transforming an idea into a reality. Last, I would be remiss if I did not make special note of my appreciation to Suzanne LaRosa, a cofounder of NewSouth Books, now an imprint of UGA Press, for her belief in this project when it was originally proposed to her during the transition of NewSouth to UGA. All these people and more helped shepherd this from concept to completion, and I am in their debt.

This Southern Metropolis

INTRODUCTION

Two deeply held and closely related personal interests that have influenced my professional career and consumed no little of my leisure time—the study of history and a love of travel—inspired this book. I have worked with a variety of cultural heritage institutions, ranging from archives and museums to historical societies and parks, since I graduated from college. The most basic commonality in all my work has been a commitment to the study of the past and its interpretation for the public. Whether I am organizing collections of historic documents; mounting exhibits of rare artifacts; conducting research into the stories of local people, places, and events for publication; or conducting tours and arranging materials for interpretive panels, markers, and brochures, I have spent my working life immersed in the past of particular places. Given that an effort to engage the general public has always driven my work, a vital part of most of my projects has also been to describe the time and place under discussion so that guests and readers may better understand the information presented.

I have always enjoyed traveling and experiencing new places, and my work has allowed me to help people visit locales both figuratively and literally. Whether I am helping people visualize what life was like long ago or explore a city or region by pointing them to significant structures and sites evocative of a unique heritage, I have found that the field of history is inextricably associated with intellectual and physical tourism. Something about exploring new environments is endlessly interesting and in many ways fundamental to the human experience. Understanding something of the essence of any place one visits, though—whether it still exists or not—requires grasping something of its context.

Through a narrative based on published visitor accounts of the physical and social environment of antebellum Mobile, in this book I have attempted to help people travel to another time and place long gone. I believe travel narratives of this period are among the most evocative extant descriptions of places. Travel writing was once a popular genre in the publishing industry, perhaps never more popular than during the first half of the nineteenth century. The style and format had become somewhat standardized by then, and steam-powered river and rail transportation made touring expansive regions possible in a way that simply was not even imaginable only a few decades earlier. Travel has always been expensive, however, and only a small percentage of the population had the resources and free time to satisfy their curiosity during extended leisure visits to various locations. This did not mean people were uninterested in reading about faraway places. Thousands of people purchased narratives of tours through the United States, the countries of Europe, and other locations around the globe in the nineteenth century, with some of the most popular works going through multiple printings. These volumes brought to life places that many people found of interest but that relatively few would get a chance to see themselves.

The authors of travel narratives became their readers' tour guides. Therefore the writers sought out even small things that made one place markedly different from another so they could better characterize a particular location and keep the story they were telling lively. Writers who hoped to publish their travel journals sought to answer the questions they anticipated readers would have. These authors were often actively looking for things that struck them as noteworthy and singular about a place and made an effort to capture the essence of a locale in its physical and cultural reality. Such narratives thus represent, in a sense, some notion of how the outside world perceived a place.

While a detailed history of Mobile is unnecessary here, some overview of the community's storied past is appropriate because it explains, at least in part, why it became a place of note in the antebellum era. Founded in 1702 by the French at a site upriver from its current location (it moved to its contemporary setting in 1711), during its first one hundred years Mobile was a colorful but struggling frontier outpost. The French, British, and Spanish occupied it in succession, each planning for it to become something more than it did, but they left a unique international imprint on the city and its surrounding areas. In 1813, at the height of the War of 1812 and after U.S. citizens and officials had lobbied for years for the city's incorporation in an American territory, it at last became a U.S. possession upon being seized from Spain, along with part of West Florida, by forces under the command

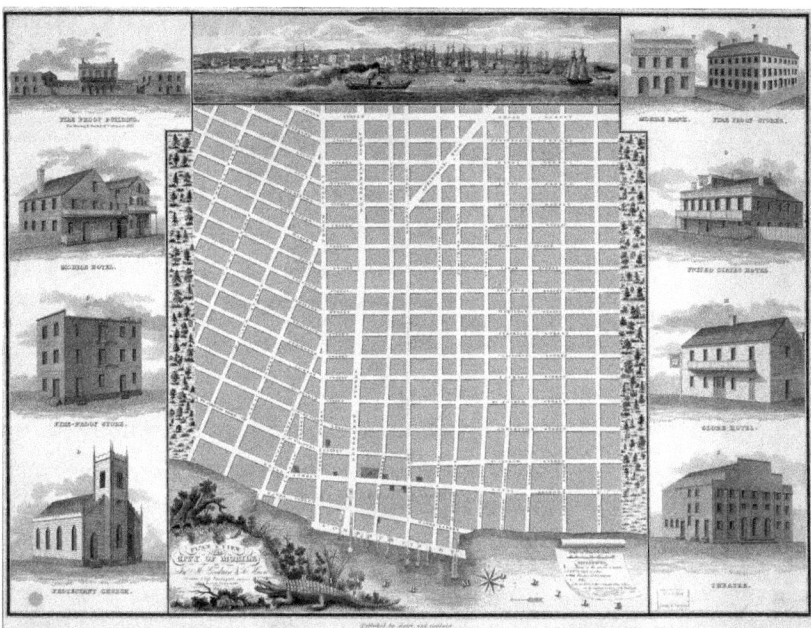

Map of Mobile in 1824 by Goodwin and Haire. Courtesy of the Library of Congress.

of General James Wilkinson. In April 1813, Mobile and environs became annexed to the Mississippi Territory. Thus ended the rich and diverse colonial era of 111 years and opened an era of dynamic growth in population and economic influence.

Even at the height of its development in its early American period, Mobile, as other writers have pointed out, can best be described as "an old town but a young city." So while "spectacular growth, reckless prosperity, and a heady sense of optimism" characterized the city's early development, so did the rough-and-tumble of a trading community growing up in what might be viewed as America's southwestern frontier. Rowdy, unpolished, and coming fully to life only during the fall and winter cotton-trading season, the town seemed more a place of promise than a destination during the first few decades of American control, first as a part of the Mississippi Territory and then upon Alabama's statehood in 1819. Soon enough, the city became a vital part of the new state's social, political, and economic life, and Mobile took on aspects of refinement that marked its arrival. In the words of one of Mobile's most beloved chroniclers, Caldwell Delaney, "in the 1840s and 1850s... Mobile became a city." Newspapers, schools, churches, stores, hotels, theaters, markets, and infrastructure, including water systems, gas lights, and paved streets, took shape. Militias, fire companies, civic groups, mutual aid societies, and a wide variety of other new organizations met public needs, drew together those with shared interests, and collectively became one measure of the city's arrival.[1]

Mobile exhibited phenomenal growth in the second half of the antebellum era. Its population increased a staggering 1,000 percent in the years between 1830 and 1860. About 60 percent of Alabama's urban population resided in Mobile by 1860, when it stood as the state's largest city several times over. At a time when only five communities in Alabama had populations of more than twenty-five hundred residents, Mobile's nearly thirty thousand inhabitants made the city a veritable metropolis in comparison. Mobile's people were as diverse as they were numerous during its antebellum heyday. In addition to being home to the largest white population in the state, the city hosted a mix of free Black, foreign-born, and Creole communities rivaled only by New Orleans's at the time. Mobile was also home to thousands of enslaved people. The institution of slavery pervaded every aspect of life in antebellum Alabama and lay at the core of the economic activity that fueled Mobile's growth. Its port flourished, a direct result of the trade in cotton that enslaved people produced, processed, and helped transport from the field to the market.[2]

Mobile's location, at the mouth of large river systems that drain an enormous expanse of some of the best arable land on the continent and at the head of a bay that empties into the Gulf of Mexico, allowed the city to become one of the busiest and most important trading centers in the nation. But its strategic position also made it a hub for both leisure and business travel by a wide range of individuals throughout the nation and beyond, as it connected much of the Deep South with the open ocean and, from there, other coastal locations in the United States, Mexico, the Caribbean, and the nations of South America and Europe, among others. In short, antebellum Mobile enjoyed a regional preeminence during an era that, in a variety of ways, made it a place visitors wanted and needed to see to understand the region and a place visitors would pass through because of its centrality in southern waterborne transportation networks.

Numerous books describe Mobile's robust history. Alabama's oldest city, and for much of its history its largest, is perhaps the most studied community in the state in terms of the sheer number of books focusing on its past. Many of these original works were invaluable as I investigated the city's nineteenth-century heritage. The authors to whom I am indebted include Harriet Amos Doss, *Cotton City: Urban Development in Antebellum Mobile;* Elizabeth Barrett Gould, *From Fort to Port: An Architectural History of Mobile, Alabama, 1711–1918;* John Sledge, *The Mobile River;* Michael V. R. Thomason, ed., *Mobile: The New History of Alabama's First City,* and a host of other historians of the city, from Caldwell Delaney to Jay Higginbotham.

This book is not an attempt to provide a thorough summary of all aspects of life in the pre–Civil War city. Rather, I have tried to help readers understand important, overarching themes of life in Mobile at the time by exploring features of its built and social environment that well-traveled visitors believed best distinguished it from other American communities of the time. Its chapters are arranged by grouping together the most common themes addressed in their writing. I have provided contextual information to help readers better understand what the authors of the travel narratives were attempting to describe. Some visitors whose experiences are captured here loved the place. Fredrika Bremer, who exclaimed in her account that "I like Mobile, and the people of Mobile, and the weather of Mobile, and every thing in Mobile; I flourish in Mobile." Some hated it. Charles A. Clinton professed, "There is nothing attractive in the aspect of Mobile." But few judged the city to be either entirely wondrous or wretched. Most visitors simply recorded their observations of the city as they encountered it and moved on to the next spot in their journey. When they put pen to paper to try to describe what made antebellum Mobile stand out, however, they created a collective body of work that records the city during an era of growth and transformation. While their accounts provide only a snapshot of life in the town at any given moment, the illumination they provide makes it possible to see a broader reality that might otherwise lie undiscovered or underappreciated.[3]

I endeavored to answer for readers two fundamental questions that reveal this book's scope, purpose, and relevance: Who were the people who wrote about antebellum Mobile? Why did I focus on the antebellum period at all? Of the more than sixty accounts I gathered, about 90 percent were written by men, nearly half of whom hailed from northern European countries, and

The English sociologist Harriet Martineau—educated, well traveled, and a capable writer—was the type of observer whose written descriptions nineteenth-century readers sought. From *The Masterpiece Library of Short Stories*, 1873.

all, as far as I am able to discern, were white. Virtually all who worked held what we would call white-collar positions; among them were politicians, ministers, educators, actors, musicians, business owners, and, of course, writers. Without doubt, this is not a diverse assemblage of authors and as such a homogeneous group they were unlikely to provide the perspectives of all Mobilians in their writing. In any case, none professed it to be their mission. Also, these visitors were almost always in town for only a few days and during their stays concentrated on the most prominent public spaces and perhaps the interiors of a few homes of well-heeled hosts. But the same set of limitations must be considered when dealing with any set of published accounts of just about any community of the era. So long as we understand this and take into consideration what the accounts can and cannot tell us, I believe they nonetheless have a lot to say that is worth our attention. Written by literate, well-traveled guests purposefully seeking out the singular aspects of a place, published travel narratives highlight what residents might regard as commonplace. They are informative and entertaining even if they do not paint the whole picture of Mobile at the time; they do help frame the canvas and color in some of the defining features of the community as it once existed.

As to why I focus exclusively on the antebellum era, the answer is simple. The period is not only a foundational epoch in the city's past but one that stood in marked contrast to other periods in its long history. Mobile held a strategic position in colonial North America during the more than one hundred years it was occupied by French, British, and Spanish authorities it became part of the United States in 1813. But more than that, the larger region has never regained the prestige, population, and economic might it attained between 1813 and 1861, when the Civil War began. Mobile's antebellum years were decades of nearly continual, dynamic growth during which the city morphed from a contested colonial backwater into one of the largest and most diverse economic powerhouses in the South. By 1860, Mobile's nearly thirty thousand inhabitants made it the fourth most populous city in what would become the Confederacy. Within the Gulf Coast region it stood second only to New Orleans in population, wealth, and influence. But the antebellum era also is important for reasons that are less easy to quantify. The period in some ways defined the outside world's view of Mobile for generations, and that notion of the city, both in its physical reality and in suppositions about life within it at the time, remain today a vital part of our understanding of the essence of the place. Further, the themes that come to the fore when studying antebellum Mobile are fundamental to understanding its unique sense of place. How would one describe Mobile, even in contemporary times, without addressing its past and the heritage that shaped its development? How can we understand the city without coming to terms with its long history as one of the nation's busiest centers of maritime trade? How is one to understand the city's physical development without discussing the era during which some of its hallmark structures—hundreds of homes and businesses—were erected? Is it possible to describe Mobile without reference to its physical setting alongside the Mobile River and at the head of venerable Mobile Bay? How can we understand Mobile's cultural history without a discussion of its unusual population mix—not only whites but Creole and free Black communities, enslaved people, and the largest immigrant population in the state—when the city first rose to prominence in the decades before the Civil War? The visitor accounts on which this book is based provide one avenue for addressing all these fundamental questions about Mobile's past. I hope you will find them as entertaining and intriguing as I did and come to a better understanding of this important era in the city's history.

CHAPTER 1

Getting There

A wearisome passage of forty-eight hours, diversified only by protracted stoppages at the various landing-places.
—Louis F. Tasistro

Wherever the eye rested, it was on cotton.
—John Guy Vassar

Mobile is located at the mouth of one of the nation's largest river systems, where the waters of the Alabama and Tombigbee Rivers and their tributaries drain a region of more than forty-four thousand square miles across portions of four states and empty into Mobile Bay. Many visitors to antebellum Mobile whose observations are included in this book arrived in the city by steamboat along this vast river system. The most popular and convenient form of long-distance transportation in the region in the first half of the nineteenth century, steamboats offered travelers opportunities for relatively speedy travel between port cities; overland travel could be considerably more difficult and unpredictable. Taking a journey by steamboat could be an experience unto itself, and the trip across regional waterways formed some of the most memorable parts of the trip for many.

The steamboat came of age and reached its height of popularity in the decades before the Civil War. It represented nothing less than a transportation revolution that facilitated commerce and travel on a scale previously unknown. At the beginning of Mobile's American era, flatboats and keelboats, moving at the speed of the current downstream and laboriously pulled back upstream with ropes or cables, were the only effective way to travel long distances on regional waterways. Making the downriver trip from Montgomery to Mobile could take perhaps two weeks in the early 1810s, and returning by the same route proved prohibitive for all but the most determined. Covering the distance between the cities going upstream could take at least a month and sometimes two. When the first steamboats arrived on the rivers of Alabama in the late 1810s, they heralded a revolution in transportation that would transform Mobile into a trade and tourism destination. The speed and ease of travel were remarkable, and the city and the surrounding region embraced the new technology wholeheartedly. By 1818 steamboats were being constructed in the Mobile area, and as early as 1821 two steamboat manufacturing companies had been established in Mobile itself. In short order, dozens of boats were operating on the rivers connecting Mobile Bay with the interiors of Alabama and Mississippi. By 1840 more than seventy boats were in regular operation out of the port of Mobile, and some of them, in the words of one traveler, were "fine high-pressure steamers."[1]

Regular service between Mobile, Montgomery, and New Orleans was established early in the antebellum period. Prices of course varied during the more than four decades chronicled here, but passage between these cities could generally be purchased for five to fifteen dollars, depending on the boat and the type of accommodations offered. Throughout most of this period, travelers could expect to cover the distance between Montgomery and Mobile in forty to fifty hours. The pace varied according to the speed of the current and whether a boat was moving upriver or down, but an average speed ranged from six to sixteen miles per hour, with frequent stops for fuel and cargo a matter of course. Some visitors arrived on steamboats from New Orleans. Their journeys involved either traveling down the Mississippi River and across the Gulf of Mexico or passing through Lake Borgne and skirting the coast before entering Mobile Bay and traversing its thirty miles of open water. The latter route took approximately the same amount of time as the trip from Montgomery. By 1850 a daily connection between New Orleans and Mobile ran across the waters of the Gulf, weather permitting.[2]

Even a top speed of sixteen miles per hour, which strikes the modern reader as anything but swift, proved dramatically faster than overland travel. The Scottish geologist Charles Lyell recounted in his journal his experience in Alabama in the 1840s, after people advised him it was preferable and safer to take the round trip of more than five hundred miles by water between Tuscaloosa and Mobile than to suffer the one hundred miles of primitive road from Tuscaloosa to Montgomery to catch a steamer to Mobile. The Swedish businessman and diplomat C. D. Arfwedson received the same advice when inquiring about the best way to get from New Orleans to Mobile in the early

1830s. "I was continually dissuaded from proceeding by mail [stagecoach] to New Orleans, on account of the badness of the road," he remembered, "and was recommended to proceed by sea."[3]

Steamboats of the day were at once utilitarian conveyances and spectacular machinery that overwhelmed the senses of travelers. The boats were often more than two hundred feet long with multiple decks and could carry hundreds of passengers or thousands of bales of cotton. Steamboats were big, noisy, floating spectacles. Berths for passengers, sometimes numbering in the dozens, usually flanked the main decks. Men's and women's parlors were commonly located on opposite sides of the boat, with their occupants customarily meeting only at meals. A host of workers with specific, essential tasks labored aboard the boats. Roustabouts and stevedores handled the loading and offloading of cargo; firemen and engineers tended to the engines; stewards set up and moved furniture and served meals that cooks had prepared; clerks kept records and handled finances; pilots and the captain navigated.[4]

The unique auditory sensation of the enormous steam engines that powered these vessels was among the first things travelers noted in their accounts of journeys to and from Mobile. Viewing the boat he was to take, one visitor at the landing admitted that the high-pressure steam engine and the "thundering rush of steam, vomited through her capacious pipes, rather startled me the first time I heard it." Another remarked on the "most unearthly sound, like that of a huge monster gasping for breath" made by the boat as it lay at the dock in preparation for a voyage. Others remembered more pleasant sounds they associated with steamboats. One such traveler arrived at the dock in Montgomery for a trip downriver to find the "air was filled with the music of a steam organ on one of the boats, which was played by a German musical artist, engaged by the year, at a handsome salary. It is a strange music that fills the air with a vast body of harmony, carrying with it the impression of the power that gives it birth—in the range of long cylindrical boilers—of which the organ is the melodious collection of escape pipes and safety valves." Once the boat was under way, the engines formed a constant acoustic and physical backdrop to the voyage. Not only were they noisy pieces of machinery, but while in operation they literally shook the interior of the boat with what one person described as a "tremulous motion communicated by the high-pressure engine, through all this range of cabins . . . so great as to render it almost impossible to write, and very difficult even to hold a book steady enough to read."[5]

A variety of other sounds accompanied steamboat travel. One passenger recalled sharing space aboard his boat with a noisy cargo of turkeys and geese while journeying downriver to Mobile. "I can very well remember the squawking, cackling, and gobbling of the feathered cargo, intermingled with some cursing of the crew," he wrote. At least in some instances, however, the audio accompaniment to cruises proved more pleasant. The journalist Hiram Fuller remembered that on a journey he took on Alabama rivers, among the passengers was "a lady who sings divinely" and provided her cohorts with "a blessed relief from the dull monotony of the river, the Kansas talk of the men, and the smaller talk of the women."[6]

Travelers who took passage on one of these technological marvels almost always commented on similar experiences in their written accounts. Their observations belie any contemporary notions of the grace and grandeur of river travel in the antebellum days. The writers noted the variety and quality of the furniture on the decks—from sofas and rocking chairs to dining tables—and the number and size of the passenger berths. But they also noted that crowded conditions seemed to have been the norm, with operators then as now seeking to maximize profits while meeting a high demand for their services. With "every room, berth, and cot taken," remarked one traveler to Mobile, the boat he took became one mass "confusion of voices, confusion of baggage, confusion of faces, and confusion of feelings." The chroniclers decried the typically mediocre meals served at community tables, the sometimes dirty plates and utensils on which they were served, and the coarse manners of many of the passengers they encountered. Many found the overall experience less than enchanting. "I was glad to leave the boat," one man remembered, "which was a very dirty concern, and nothing could be less tempting than our fare; some of the passengers were kind and communicative, but others were too fond of gambling, and spitting, and smoking to permit the enjoyment of much comfort."[7]

Indeed, the manners and habits of the other passengers aboard steamers bound for Mobile provoked much comment in the accounts of visitors to the city. Many noted how frequently they found themselves in the company of businessmen from the South who were traveling to "make their spring purchases, or Northern men returning from a business tour to the South." Travelers often described these guests as well dressed but "drinking a great deal" (to the authors' dissatisfaction). Some considered these guests drunken boors, several described them as "exceedingly offensive both in habits and deportment," and "coarse in their manners, and in many instances very disgusting." The propensity of some passengers to engage in gambling to while away the trip proved equally offensive to many. Although we tend to think of the drinking and gambling as going hand in hand, some travelers were surprised to see so many passengers were "members of a society established in the Southern and Western States, whose occupation is exclusively directed to gambling pursuits." The problem most associated with gambling seems not to have been the games themselves but the violence that accompanied arguments about money among men who had been drinking. In the estimation of one traveler, it seemingly became the gamers' "delight, and at other times their object, for reasons best known to themselves, to create disturbances amongst the passengers, which, in these fiery latitudes, are so often fatal to those who are implicated." Drinking and gambling proved to be so common aboard steamboats that their absence became occasions of note for some travelers. One man recalled his profound surprise to have encountered "only one drunken man, and not a card seen during the passage" during his 1846 trip between Mobile and Montgomery.[8]

Even more obnoxious, in the eyes of the travelers whose accounts are featured here, was the ubiquitous use of tobacco aboard steamers. Everyone, women included, seemed to use tobacco products. "The white lady citizens . . . here and there, still have a custom of seeking for a higher life's enjoyment by rubbing their gums with snuff, which produces a sort of intoxication very stimulating to the feelings, and to the conversation likewise." Another traveler-writer came across a particularly colorful character who doubled down on his use of the leaf when questioned. "Tobacco is as necessary to me as it is agreeable," he boasted. "I have chewed since I was knee high to a goose, and will go on chewing until I'm a gone goose."[9]

Because of the relative speed of river travel, passengers were for the most part willing to tolerate the many inconveniences. However, trips on steamboats could still involve numerous maddening delays. The boat stopped—sometimes as often as every five to ten miles—at the dozens of riverside landings to restock wood for the engine boilers, perhaps to take on a few passengers, and to load ever more cotton. The stops vexed travelers and turned the boats into nothing less than floating cotton barges. Hence, as one traveler observed, a trip between Montgomery and Mobile formed "a wearisome passage of forty-eight hours, diversified only by protracted stoppages at the various landing-places, and through a wild and uninteresting country." It was not uncommon to stop twenty times or more—'at every river cliff,' in the words of one weary traveler—between central Alabama and Mobile.[10]

The procedure for loading cotton formed a sort of entertaining diversion for a few steamboat passengers. Workers transferred bales from the riverbank onto the deck of the boat by means of a "long and steeply-inclined plane . . . cut in the high bank, down which one heavy bale after another is made to slide." The process was particularly memorable at night. The Irish stage actor Tyrone Power (1797–1841) remembered that during his trip along the Alabama River in the 1830s, his boat took on cotton late in the evening at one stop. "An animated sight in a dark night," he recorded, "is the sliding down of cotton bales from a high bluff, while camp fires are lighted on the banks, and the five or six furnace doors on the main deck are thrown open, and the red glare of light throws its lurid beams upon the gangs of negroes, singing sailor songs." However interesting the process might have been, by its fifteenth or so iteration on the same trip, it had become tiresome. By the time the boats reached their destination after taking on cargo several times, they were often "a floating mass of cotton." By the time they pulled into Mobile, passengers noted, "wherever the eye rested, it was on cotton." The bales blocked windows and narrowed the passageways. Many travelers aboard regional steamers would remember the unique sensation of being surrounded by a haze of cotton lint as the boat proceeded along the river. Even the few passengers taken aboard at the landings became preoccupied with cotton, and it became their "sole topic" of conversation, according to an exasperated British visitor named Basil Hall. Another veteran of steamboat travel between Montgomery and Mobile remembered the entire length of the Alabama River as little more than "a muddy river, whose banks were strewn with bales of cotton."[11]

The numerous navigation hazards within river channels made travel more harrowing than many would have liked. Low water levels presented a formidable obstacle that forced boats to stop at night rather than try to navigate

Although steamboats were built for utilitarian purposes, their interiors could be ornate. This image of a Tombigbee steamboat dining hall, taken in the latter part of the nineteenth century, shows the extravagance that river travelers enjoyed. Courtesy of the Alabama Department of Archives and History (ADAH).

Voyages along the Tombigbee and Alabama river systems usually required multiple stops at dozens of landings for additional fuel, water, passengers, and cotton. To facilitate loading from the high riverbanks, some locations featured chutes for sliding bales from the bluff to the boat deck. Courtesy of ADAH.

This sketch depicts the work at the bottom of the chutes: securing and positioning the heavy bales to maximize the number taken aboard. Courtesy of ADAH.

treacherous shallows without adequate light. Shallow waters in the bay made travel just as dicey on occasion. Boats sometimes ran aground when certain weather conditions lowered water levels in a bay whose primary navigation channel was less than twelve feet deep. "We got a-ground for half an hour," recounted one frustrated traveler who regarded it as part of the experience since he knew it could have been much worse. Maritime travelers and crew were well aware of the snags known as sinkers and sawyers—trees stuck in the river bottom and perched to rip open hulls of the wooden boats passing over them—a terror that lurked throughout the navigable reaches of regional rivers. Captains had to be always on the lookout for these perils and others, for even floating debris such as logs and large limbs could do serious damage when struck at speed. High water presented an entirely different sort of vexation. The overflowing banks of swift-moving rivers filled with debris might bring boats closer to the tree line than usual and played havoc with the crude steering systems of most steamboats. The consequence often was limbs that scraped the sides of boats and broke windows while the boat was traversing narrow bends. "Whilst at dinner," one passenger headed toward Mobile recounted, "a huge branch burst open a side door, and nearly impaled a French conjurer of celebrity on his way to New Orleans." A British visitor, Robert Russell, remembered how his boat became entangled in a "grove of willows" in a period of high water. The boat sustained only minor damage, but the event no doubt raised the heart rates of all aboard.[12]

At the top of the list of feared dangers loomed boiler explosions and fires that might mean instant death or leave one on the open water with no good options. Knowledge of these explosions haunted the back corners of travelers' minds and for good reason. The temperamental nature of steam engine technology of the day, and the inexact science of determining critical variables in their operation, yielded dangerous circumstances above and beyond river conditions. The accumulation of mud from river water could clog sensitive engine mechanisms and might lead to overheating, for example. Avoiding this potentially fatal problem required specialized knowledge and quick reaction. The threat of a sudden inferno was real and not just from overheating. Vessels were frequently carrying hundreds of bales of flammable cotton, and the smokestacks of their boilers sometimes emitted showers of sparking embers.

These factors of operation, combined with the premiums placed on speed and profitability and minimal laws addressing steamboat safety, were often a recipe for disaster. Cautionary tales of steamboat boiler explosions and fires loomed large in river travel of the day. Tales of the horrific loss of life were somewhat akin to the terrifying air travel disasters of our modern era for their randomness and the helplessness of passengers caught up in them. The 1836 boiler explosion of the *Ben Franklin*, which occurred while the boat sat at Mobile's dock, was one of several devastating accidents that many river travelers could not help but think of. The explosion killed about fifteen and wounded a dozen more while scattering body fragments across the riverfront. In 1847, in another widely publicized disaster, the *Tuscaloosa*'s boilers exploded near Twelve Mile Island, north of the city, on a cold and stormy January night. Some passengers were scalded by the boiling water that gushed over the decks; others drowned in the icy waters. One of the greatest maritime disasters in local history—one that haunts regional memory to this day—occurred when the *Eliza Battle* burned on a remote stretch of the flooded Tombigbee on a bitterly cold March night in 1858. The boat caught fire while carrying hundreds of bales of cotton and dozens of passengers. Nearly three dozen people died, and many of those who survived did so only by making their way out of the frigid waters and clinging to the tops of the half-submerged trees that stood in the fast-moving river. One visitor to antebellum Mobile remembered seeing the ill-fated *Eliza Battle* at the city wharf shortly before the disaster and afterward wrote how "this elegant steamer, a floating palace ... was suddenly discovered to be on fire in her voyage from Mobile up the Tombigbee." He then recounted what he had heard of the terrible experience of those who lived and the tragic deaths of others. All these and other disasters became especially visceral and immediate when passengers observed the remains of sunken boats in the river or a problem with the boilers caused a temporary panic.[13]

Traversing the Gulf on open water route to Mobile from New Orleans could be fraught with some of these and other types of troubles. In any vessel the Gulf's notoriously unpredictable waters posed danger from storms and swells. But some of the shallow-bottomed transports that made the trip were not designed for windswept, choppy waters. More than one tourist got caught on rough water, which made them seasick at best and fearful for their life at worst. "The evening was beautiful when we left Mobile, although the breeze made the water rather rougher than suited the construction of some of the female stomachs," recalled one traveler who took a boat with her family to New Orleans after a visit to Mobile. Because of the rough waters, the boat she was on anchored for the night near Dauphin Island before entering the Gulf. Even so, she recalled "tossing the whole night in the most wretched manner possible throughout a violent storm of wind, lightning, and some rain." Daylight and clearing skies brought stronger winds. "The morning came," she noted, but "once more we moved on against a violent head wind which made a sea fit to tear anyone's stomach to atoms." The British scientist George Featherstonhaugh, traveling between the Gulf Coast cities in the 1840s, encountered a small storm in the Gulf that caused him to be concerned about much more than a bit of motion sickness. He was sure the maelstrom would overturn the little steamer he was aboard and wrote of how, during his harrowing journey, he thought "the day of reckoning had arrived." More than one traveler who ventured across the open waters of the Gulf reported

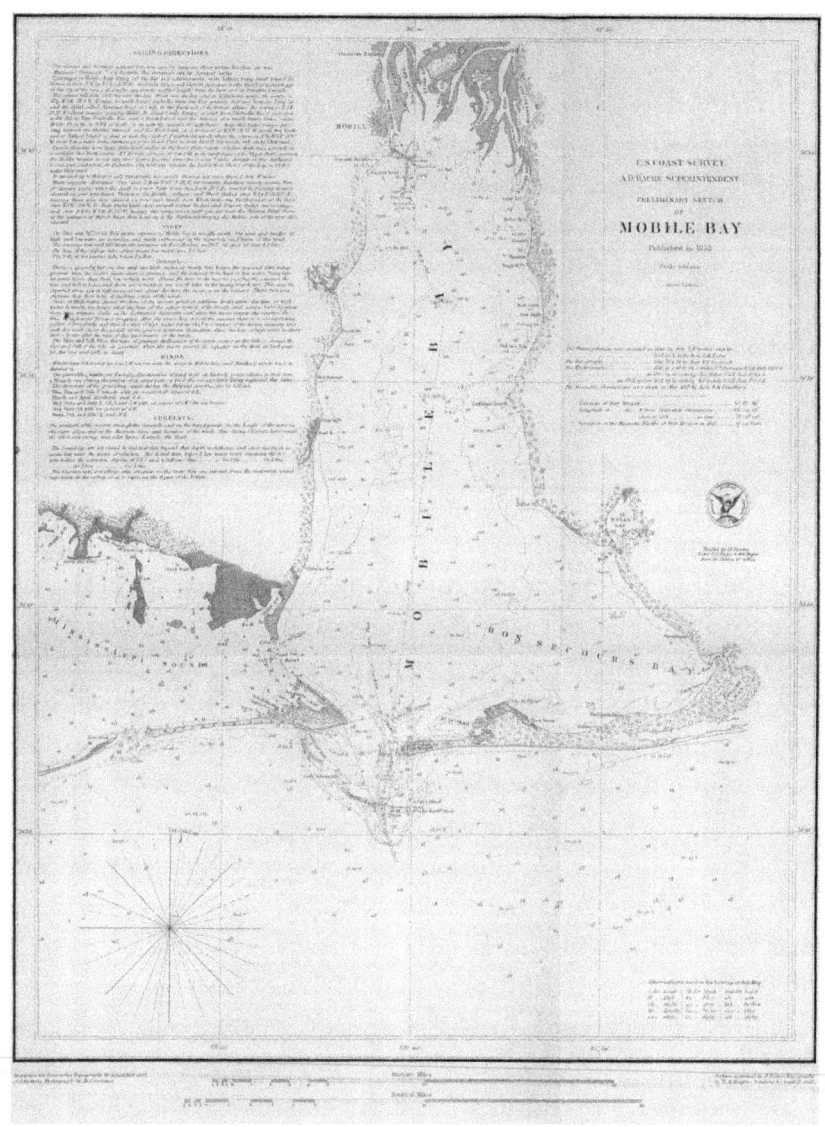

This chart of Mobile Bay by A. D. Bache, produced in 1852, contains detailed information about how to navigate it during the antebellum period. It shows depths throughout, as well as the main channel and upper and lower anchorages for fleets. Courtesy of the David Rumsey Map Collection.

being happy when at last they found themselves "within the bay of Mobile, and pressing over its smooth waters."[14]

Sightseeing guests on their way to Mobile tried to pass the time by taking in the scenery. Depictions of the area that appeared in travel narratives ranged from lackluster and depressing to extraordinary and serene. Many panned the scenery along the Alabama River as "of the most uninviting and monotonous character," with several agreeing to various degrees with one traveler who thought the brown waters of the stream might appropriately be called "liquid-mud." In a particularly vivid description of what he regarded as altogether unsightly, John Shaw summarized what he saw on a trip downriver from central Alabama by declaring, "This river and the alligator are well matched; for I think it would be with difficulty that one could encounter two uglier things in the domains of universal nature." Those who traversed the waters of the Tensaw, the stream that roughly parallels the Mobile River south of where the Alabama and the Tombigbee join it and that delineates the eastern boundary of the delta, likewise shared mixed opinions of the scenery. The British writer and botanist Amelia Murray, who had visited Georgia shortly before arriving in southern Alabama, pronounced the Tensaw to be "a stream [as] beautiful as the Altamaha, and bordered by woods far exceeding those of Georgia." She sometimes saw "huge alligators . . . basking beneath these verdant shores and elegant birds flying above them." Other travelers were less intrigued by Tensaw's natural abundance, proclaiming it to merely be "a winding stream through a flat country, in some parts narrow, with alligator swamps on each side."[15]

For every writer who expressed disappointment with the views leading to Mobile, however, many more were captivated while traversing the rivers' lower reaches. "The scenery on the Alabama River is beautiful and in many places very wild and romantic," remembered one visitor. The American writer Joseph Holt Ingraham seconded the thought, proclaiming the river romantic and recalling his trip fondly in his account of a visit to the region. A pair of Hungarian sisters, Francis and Theresa Pulszky, deemed the trip along the Alabama River among the most scenic in all their travels, exulting, "We have scarcely yet made a more picturesque tour in the United States. . . . Here for the first time we felt ourselves amidst primitive nature." Nighttime travel could be particularly enchanting. In the evening, one visitor wrote, one had the opportunity to experience a "still and dream-like... landscape," with moonlight illuminating "the fairy solitude of wood and flood, [so] that it seemed as if we had passed the uttermost confines of civilization."[16]

The rivers filled and charmed the senses of many, with one recounting the solemnity of floating downstream surrounded by nature's beauty as the "faint land-breeze is loaded with the odours of the jessamine [jasmine], which now fills the forests with its blossoms, and floods the whole air with its fragrance." The naturalist Phillip Henry Gosse expressed the thoughts of many who became enraptured by the beauty they found in "the calm, mirror-like surface, unruffled by a zephyr, [that] gives back the light of each individual star." This despite interruptions at regular intervals by the "hoarse and hollow booming of the steam" from the boat's engines. Gosse sat up late during his downriver voyage, observing with delight the bats and whippoorwills he saw from his window as they made their nocturnal rounds. Several others were struck by the splendor of the river at night in calm conditions when the water became one vast reflecting pool. "I was peculiarly struck with the beauty of the stars reflected in the pure waters of the river," Thomas Hamilton observed in the early 1830s. "The whole sky was mirrored with a vividness which exceeded every thing of the kind I have ever witnessed before or since." Even inclement weather had a special kind of beauty, according to a visitor who during a voyage one evening could see storms looming in the distance. "The night is beautiful.... The sky is continually illuminated by flashes of lightning, that play along the edge of the horizon." Another enchanted traveler recalled that, "long after all the rest of the passengers had retired to rest, I continued on deck with unabated delight; and when I retired, it was not to sleep, for I could not avoid sitting up in bed, and gazing, through the open window of my berth, on the placid beauty of the night."[17]

CHAPTER 2

Arrival

There are sometimes from thirty to sixty vessels lying at anchor in the bay . . . all busily loading or disgorging their cargoes—a sight which is well calculated to impress the tourist with the commercial importance of the place.
—*Alexander Mackay*

The prospect of getting once more into a comfortable house, was too great not to be grasped at. If any one thinks otherwise I recommend him a fort-nights journey through the Southern States of America.
—Basil Hall

Some visitors' most vivid recollections of Mobile were their first impressions of the city, formed as they drew near, docked at its wharf, and began their exploration of its streets. Whether they entered Mobile's harbor from the river or approached it by traveling up the bay, reminders that the place was a busy commercial port—in the form of vessels of all shapes and sizes—abounded long before they could see the city itself. This experience helped guests form an opinion of the place even before they walked its streets. But their first few moments in the city, spent seeking out accommodations, formed another principal part of their estimation of the community.

Antebellum Mobile, with its low-slung buildings and waterfront lined with wharves and docks, did not loom above the surrounding marsh in the way the skyscrapers of modern downtown are visible for miles around. In fact, several visitors arriving at Mobile by water in the first half of the nineteenth century remarked on how hidden the city seemed to be, nestled along the riverfront amid "boundless swamps," surrounded "on every other side" by tall reeds. "Its approach is disfigured by marshy land, covered with old logs, and the forests crowd close upon the city," wrote one tourist, Joseph Holt Ingraham. "Mobile does not come into view until we are close upon it," remarked a typical account, noting the city lay "hidden behind a wooded cape or projection." If they noticed that their impressions were at odds with descriptions of the city in various guidebooks of the era—for example, the

Traveller's Tour described the city as "situated on Mobile river . . . built in a high and commanding situation"—this went unremarked. Thick riverside forests stood between the river and the flat plain on which the city's grid of streets had been carved. One traveler approaching by night remarked how, as his steamer neared the port, he could discern the extent of Mobile's homes and businesses (few of which had more than two stories) "chiefly by their lights," which faintly penetrated the gloom.[1]

As a boat neared the docks, the heart of the city, with its businesses, churches, and scattered homes, at last came into full view. Antebellum Mobile's waterfront was a gritty, bustling zone dedicated to commerce, with wharves and dozens of warehouses and other commercial structures near the river. Just beyond lay streets crowded with stores, with a church punctuating the modest skyline here and there. "As we drew nearer, the towers and spires had a pretty effect," observed a typical visitor. Many were taken aback by the abrupt contrast between the city and the surrounding terrain, which truly seemed to be an island of urban development amid a vast watery world. But what drew the most comment were the dramatic signs of activity on the water that served as the city's lifeblood. Ships lay anchored or were approaching and leaving Mobile from multiple directions. "Many steamers . . . were clustered about the wharves, and square-rigged vessels . . . were seen at anchor beyond," one writer remembered. Another recalled gazing southward from the city into the bay, where he not only beheld "a handsome view of Mobile Bay" but "counted nine ships of various sizes stretching in."[2]

For many of those approaching the city from the bay or traversing its length on the way to their next stop, the bay provided some of the most memorable maritime scenes and lasting images of Mobile. Despite all the activity, "only a few small craft and steamboats" used Mobile's wharves. All the seagoing vessels trading in its port anchored out in the bay and had their cargoes discharged from or transferred to them. The Dog River Bar stretches across the middle of the bay and back then allowed watercraft only seven feet of water for navigation in average conditions. This natural feature prevented large ships from reaching the city's wharves in the days before regular dredging of the channel (today it is maintained to a depth of more than forty feet, giving some of the largest ships afloat access the port). Instead, in the antebellum period oceangoing vessels would anchor in the lower bay and laboriously load cargoes from, or offload them to, a barge that would carry them out of or into Mobile's harbor. By the 1850s nearly one hundred local steamer tugs or bay boats were engaged in serving what became known as the "lower fleet"—lightering goods to and from the larger vessels. Thus it was that "the shipping lies thirty miles below" the city, as one observer noted.[3]

The floating forest of masts south of the city became a spectacle for visitors and sightseers. Most who passed it, such as the British traveler John Oldmixon, remarked on the "curious sight," observing that the assemblage of boats appeared to be nothing less than "a town of ships; a little floating community" formed by vessels "waiting for their cargoes." In fact, the bay had two primary anchorages where ships anchored to receive and discharge

The Mobile harbor as depicted in the margin of Haire and Goodwin's 1824 map of the city. Courtesy of the Library of Congress.

their cargo. One was just six miles south of the city in a relatively deep spot. It was by far the smaller of the two. The lower anchorage, called by some "the Roads," occupied even deeper water closer to the mouth of the bay and frequently held dozens of vessels at the peak of fall and winter trading season. More than one visitor estimated the area held more than one hundred vessels when their steamboat passed by. "There are sometimes from thirty to sixty vessels lying at anchor in the bay . . . all busily loading or disgorging their cargoes—a sight which is well calculated to impress the tourist with the commercial importance of the place," recalled one writer. The American historian and minister John S. C. Abbott noted with incredulity that he saw about a "hundred large ships, many of them of the first class, loading and unloading by lighters, nearly thirty miles below the city."[4]

The enormous commercial pageant impressed visitors. Ships flying American, British, and French flags lay bobbing at anchor for a distance estimated by some to be "four or five miles in each direction." Several authors commented on what they beheld as "an unusually magnificent spectacle; especially as all the ships were perfectly ready for sea, with their sails bent, top-gallant yards across, and in the highest possible order." The activity also caught visitors' attention; one noted how "to and from its anchorage plied the smoking Bay steamers, and among them sailed a graceful cutter, the vigilant watcher of the coast." Another noted that "the songs of the sailors, loading and unloading the ships, added to the life of the spectacle."[5]

Many regarded the situation as unfortunate for the commercial prospects of the city and deemed it an enormous handicap. "If Mobile had but a channel of twenty-five feet of water over her bar, she would be the great cotton city of the South," one visitor wrote, expressing a sentiment shared by several observers. A visitor who arrived during a relatively slow period for business opined, "One of the principal causes which has probably operated to effect the decline of Mobile is the obstructions to large vessels coming up to the town, a bar rendering it impossible for them to come nearer than within seven miles. If this obstruction could be removed, I think that the commercial importance of this place would again revive, and we should once more see its streets thronged with merchants. Its situation is well calculated for commerce." Others dismissed Mobile as "a waste both of time and money" and even gave "encouragement to the idea of founding another town in a better situation." As early as the 1820s, shortly after the American takeover of the city, people lobbied for deepening the channel. Senator Rufus King of Alabama led an effort to sponsor legislation to provide federal assistance to improve navigation into Mobile. Channel deepening finally began later in the decade after Blakeley was founded across the Mobile-Tensaw Delta and competed for Mobile's commerce. Between 1826 and 1839 the channel was widened to 200 feet and dredged to a depth of about ten feet. Serious long-term efforts to open a channel from the Gulf to the city for oceangoing vessels with deeper drafts would not begin until much later in the century, however.[6]

A small percentage of visitors to antebellum Mobile arrived aboard stagecoaches and missed an opportunity to observe the city's maritime navigation problems. Some were forced to consider travel by coach when low water in the rivers prohibited or delayed steamboat travel, and some sought the relative comfort of a coach, perceiving steamboat travel to be "more for the conveyance of cotton than of passengers." Coaches could be efficient methods of travel for short distances, but over long hauls they were anything but a smooth ride. Primitive springs encountering poorly maintained roads meant constant jostling, wheels and axles had a propensity to break under strain, and the vehicles became stuck with discomfiting frequency. Plus, a traveler with the misfortune of sharing the crowded quarters of a coach with an unpleasant passenger had no means of escape until arriving at their destination. One man who visited Mobile in the spring of 1830 remembered how he had been forced to endure endless hours with a man "as uncivil and rude as possible. He never opened his mouth without swearing."[7]

Most who did travel by coach arrived from the east and were then ferried across the rivers of the lower Delta to Mobile from Blakeley. Blakeley was founded immediately after the American takeover of the region in the early 1800s and briefly blossomed into a promising urban center with ambitions to rival Mobile for trade. Recurring epidemics of yellow fever, inflated real estate prices, and Mobile's getting serious about improving its harbor all combined to make Blakeley's boom a bust in only fifteen years. Adam Hodgson passed through Blakeley during its brief 1820s heyday on his way to Mobile and pronounced Blakeley "a real American town of yesterday, with a fine range of warehouses; the stumps of the trees which have been felled to make room for this young city [were] still standing in the streets." By 1830, Blakeley had entered a period of rapid decline from which it would not recover. "A few years ago Blakeley was a thriving place," remarked one visitor, "but the situation has turned out to be unhealthy, and building is now at a stand[still]." But because Blakeley remained the seat of Baldwin County and was connected by road to Stockton to the north and Pensacola to the east, it continued to be an important overland travel hub despite its downturn. A small steam-powered ferry ran between Blakeley and Mobile throughout the 1820s and 1830s. Several travelers during that era took the *Emeline* to Mobile as it made its daily trips. It was, in the words of one passenger, the "smallest steam-boat that I ever saw," built of planks and powered by a small low-pressure engine. This Lilliputian boat appeared "dirty, and the person who navigated her careless" in the estimation of the British visitor James Stuart.[8]

At least one visitor who left a published record of his journey made the trip to Mobile overland from the west. The Scottish writer Thomas Hamilton, who visited New Orleans (and other places) in the early 1830s, took a stage from Pascagoula to Mobile for the final leg of his journey before returning home. The "whole distance I observed only two houses," he recorded, "one of which was a tavern, where we stopped to sup about four in the morning. Our fare was cold venison and bacon, for which the charge was so enormous as to excite the indignation of the passengers."[9]

Even some visitors to Mobile who had arrived by boat might have wished they had opted for overland travel. Frustrating and unpredictable delays in steamboat departures could ruin a traveler's schedule and leave them almost helpless to do anything but endure the wait. Several noted that their stays in the city were delayed by a full day or more because the boat on which they had booked passage had not arrived or required some repair before leaving the port. "Waiting impatiently for a boat" is how a flustered traveler named James Davidson described a day in Mobile that he had planned to spend going back upriver to Montgomery. The next day, with the boat still nowhere in sight, Davidson confided to his journal that "I begin to hate Mobile, and know not when I can get clear of it." Unfortunately for some, delays of multiple days meant many anxious hours of peering into the Mobile River or out into the bay to see if their boat might be steaming toward the dock. They always had to be ready to go in these circumstances; if they ventured too far from the port, the boat, already behind schedule, could slip in and get away unannounced. At times like these, impatient dockside crowds carefully watched the approach of any boat to the harbor until they could confirm its identity.[10]

Perhaps even more vexing for travelers were occasions when their boat actually sat in Mobile's harbor, but unspecified delays kept it there much longer than expected. During his visit to the city in 1836, James D. Davidson recalled how during his wait he "made an acquaintance here with one who is a stranger like myself, and who is like myself waiting impatiently for a boat." When they heard that another steamer would head in the direction they needed to go one afternoon, both successfully booked passage on it. "The Captain put up his steam and induced the passengers to come on board," he remembered, but the boat did not move. Davidson sat waiting for the boat to get under way for what became interminable hours. Nothing happened and he could not discern the cause of the delay. "God only knows whether we will be off by morning or not, for the Captain does not," he noted solemnly in his journal and vowed to "try & sleep away the blues tonight." When he determined the boat would be even further delayed, he disembarked the next day and took a seat on another boat recently arrived in port. Once under way at last, he wrote sarcastically of how "I am even now tired of Mobile."[11]

Once most visitors arrived in town, they went straightaway to the hotels. Mobile had several large, good-quality boardinghouses throughout the pre–Civil War period; some ranked among the largest structures in town and became community landmarks of a sort. The Globe, the Mobile, the American, the Lafayette, Le Clede, and the Franklin House, Waverly House, and Mansion House all at various points between the 1820s and the 1850s were prominent accommodations in town. Some offered top-tier amenities and the best service of the day. Most were concentrated within an area of a few blocks bounded by Government, St. Francis, and Royal Streets. Others were nearby, for example, in the Spring Hill community west of town and along the bayfront below the city. The frequent fires that ravaged the city during the 1810s and 1820s destroyed several of these institutions and led to the construction of new facilities, some on the same spot as a predecessor. At any given time four or five of these establishments were in operation. Judging from the accounts of many guests, even that number proved insufficient to serve visitors in peak trading season.[12]

The Globe, United States, and Mobile Hotels, shown in the margins of Haire and Goodwin's 1824 map of Mobile, were representative of hotel architecture of the period. Courtesy of the Library of Congress.

The St. Michael Hotel, depicted in the margins of La Tourette's 1838 map of Mobile. Courtesy of the Library of Congress.

As I will discuss in more detail in chapter 6, Mobile's guesthouses operated seasonally in rhythm to the ebb and flow of the city's business cycles. Relatively few people chose to stay in the city during the hot and unhealthy summer and early fall. The period from the first frost (when some hotels actually opened) to the first sultry days of late spring constituted the city's business season. During this period, its population might swell to three times or more its off-season number. Mobile served as both a Gulf Coast commercial capital and winter resort. Its hotels had few rooms available (if any) during this busy travel season. Advertising good food, a large supply of high-quality liquors, and stables with adequate grain and fodder, the hotels charged what today would be extremely modest rates. In 1828 room and board at the Globe Hotel for a whole month cost twenty-four dollars ($774 in 2023). In later years visitors could expect charges of about $1.25 a day, with fifty cents or so for breakfast, and they could buy a week's worth of horse feed for about five dollars.[13]

The Battle House was by far the most well-known Mobile hotel of the era. Located at the corner of Royal and St. Francis Streets, the enterprise opened in 1852 and soon became a city landmark. The original five-story structure had more than two hundred rooms, as well as dining rooms and various shops and featured luxurious decor. Hailed as a first-class facility, it ranked among the best in the South and on par with the finest accommodations nationally. The brothers James and John Battle, along with other investors, had pooled their resources to construct the hotel on the site of the old Waverly Hotel. Work began in 1851, and it opened to the public on December 11, 1852. The Battle House quickly became among the most sought-after hotels in the city, not only for its high-class accommodations and reputation for excellent service but also for hosting a variety of social events during the busy winter season.[14]

Visitors to Mobile in the 1850s consistently gave the Battle House high marks, even if a few noted that its prices seemed a little inflated. One well-traveled visitor proclaimed the hotel to be the "best managed I have met with in the United States," while another, who traveled extensively throughout the nation during a distinguished career in theater, described it as "the best conducted and best appointed hotel in the Southern country." The hotel rated as the equal of some of the most acclaimed facilities in New York or Boston, in the estimation of Joseph Holt Ingraham, a prolific writer of the day. In his reminiscences about his time in Mobile, he declared that the Battle House stood as "a first rank American hotel. The proprietors have been very assiduous and polite to make us comfortable and we feel as much at home as if we were prince and princess in our own palace." The journalist and landscape architect Frederick Law Olmsted, among the most famous people to visit the antebellum city, noted that the Battle House stood as "an excellent hotel." The journalist Hiram Fuller found the hotel's tightly managed operation an anomaly during his travels in the southern states, describing it as, in what locals must have regarded as a backhanded compliment, "one of the very best hotels in the Union—a Southern institution with Northern principles."[15]

Overall, most visitors seemed impressed by Mobile's other hotels. In an era when good accommodations were hard to find and often amounted to

The Battle House Hotel as it appeared circa 1900, shortly before the fire that destroyed the original structure. Courtesy of the Library of Congress.

This menu from the Battle House Hotel, dating to 1857, shows the extravagant offerings and wide variety of wines available at one of Alabama's most luxurious hotels. Courtesy of the New York Public Library.

little more than a cold dirty room meant to be shared with strangers, a truly well-appointed guesthouse, something of a luxury in much of the South and a highlight of travel in the region, was sure to receive comment. "The hotels in Mobile are on a most extensive and sumptuous scale, scarcely surpassed by any of those in New York, Boston, or Philadelphia," raved one traveler. "Here is one of the best-ordered hotels in the States, and altogether as many inducements to the visitor or settler as any place I saw" was the exuberant review from another. James Silk Buckingham, visiting from England, noted that in contrast to so many places he had encountered on his American journey, his hotel in Mobile ranked as "a place of cleanliness, comfort, and repose." He also was impressed by the sheer size of some of the hotels in town. Buckingham observed the United States Hotel while it was under construction on Government Street and came away awed by its dimensions, noting that it ranked as "one of the most splendid of all the public edifices" in Mobile. When completed, he claimed, it "will be larger than the Astor House at NY, the Tremont House at Boston, or the American Hotel in Buffalo." However, before its completion the hotel was destroyed in one of the conflagrations that ravaged the city during this period.[16]

Still, a number of other visitors to Mobile documented a much less pleasant experience in the city's hotels. "My room is pretty large, but is dusty and dirty, in a sort of offshoot from the Mansion House, which is full," noted one traveler. He reported that his room had a mattress but no sheets. Another visitor found the accommodations at one hotel so wanting that he went in search of another as soon as he could. "At the first boarding house I tried at Mobile I suffered," according to his remembrances. The room and bed were cramped and uncomfortable, and the food proved unappetizing. One meal featured a centerpiece of roast pig that struck him as cruel in its presentation. "Could they [the pigs] have talked they would have said 'I am o'er young to take me from me mammy yet,'" he imagined. "And fish, oh! more like chips than fish." Margaret Hall, during a winter visit in the late 1820s with her husband, Basil, a Scottish scientist and naval officer, recounted in a letter how she had to book a room that they had to share with other guests, and it contained no fireplace. When someone unexpectedly offered Basil Hall the use of a house, he remembered that he "endeavoured to make some sort of civil answer, declining the offer—but the words stuck in my throat . . . the prospect of getting once more into a comfortable house, was too great not to be grasped at." In her letter Margaret Hall noted, "If any one thinks otherwise, I recommend him a fort-nights journey through the Southern States of America." She was overjoyed at the prospect of not having to dine again at "a noisy, bustling public table where sixty persons dispatched their unchewed dinner in the course of twenty minutes." She wrote with satisfaction how later she sat "beside a blazing fire and with the prospect of reposing on the most delicious large, firm mattress that I have seen since leaving home."[17]

Another traveler, the British artist Victoria Welby, described in detail the decrepit state of accommodations at the hotel she had booked. It seemed to her to be "extraordinarily dilapidated, every window is cracked, and every jug, glass, cup, teapot, and chair, is broken; in short, we seem to have closely followed on the steps of an earthquake or tornado!" She declared that the only respectable hotel in Mobile was "crammed full," and, although "I certainly cannot call [it] a good hotel," it had at least "a few virtues." Some new arrivals in Mobile complained less about the quality of the accommodations than their prices. Buckingham, for example, claimed charges in Mobile's hotels were as much as 50 percent higher than similar establishments he had frequented in the northern states. At least one traveler could find nothing at all redeeming about any of the hotels in Mobile and decided to shorten his stay as a result: "We left as soon as possible . . . and the next morning found ourselves in New-Orleans."[18]

The most common concern about Mobile's hotels recorded by antebellum travelers, however, was not their quality but their quantity. "It was nine o'clock in the morning when we reached Mobile," Basil Hall remembered. He wrote that he spent the first hours in town searching "in vain for rooms in the hotels." When he finally found one, he saw that the facility stood "overcrowded from top to bottom." The experience proved typical of many. "A great fire had lately destroyed the largest establishment," another traveler reported, and "the smaller ones were crowded to excess."[19]

Whether they had difficulty securing a room or regarded the accommodations posh or wretched, most visitors who left written accounts of antebellum Mobile devoted relatively few lines to their lodging. They focused most on their exploration of a city they had only glimpsed as their boat glided into port. Those observations often began with a description of the physical setting in which Mobile lay, a backdrop as different as any that most had encountered.

CHAPTER 3

The Setting

The weather was divine even in winter, and flowers of great beauty yet in abundance.
—*Tyrone Power*

As handsome an avenue as is to be seen in the country . . . lined with rows of trees on either hand, protected by an excellent flag-pavement at the sides, and already ornamented with some exceedingly handsome public structures, and private mansions and dwellings.
—*James Silk Buckingham*

Mobile's unusual natural setting caught the eye of many visitors and became the subject of much comment in their accounts of the city. For many, the city's location alone, near the mouth of a major river system and at the head of a magnificent bay, proved novel and intriguing. The lush vegetation of the area, especially the abundant variety of trees and greenery found everywhere, even in the depths of winter, seemed to fascinate a number of guests. The built environment of the city drew the attention of still others, whose commentary on the layout and quality of Mobile's streets and descriptions of its public and domestic architecture help us form a mental image of the city between 1813 and 1861.

Accounts of the city's physical setting, especially those written by people surprised by its beauty, did not stint on hyperbole. "What I had previously heard of Mobile was not very much in its favour," acknowledged the British geologist George Featherstonhaugh during his visit to the city. His journey through "the other towns in this climate," he candidly confessed, "had not raised my expectations." He came away from Mobile, however, "surprised at the peculiar beauty of the place." After a rain shower, another traveler recalled that a "repentant sunset" cast "a rose-coloured glow over everything," framing the city with a wondrous display that seemed positively romantic. The combination of fine homes along the bayside shore, the expanse of open water glimmering in the distance, and the signs of activity all around were enchanting to many. "From a light, airy, broad verandah, we might look out upon the Bay of Mobile, covered with shipping," observed one tourist who took in the view with satisfaction.[1]

Then as now, the abundance of animal life along Mobile's coast became a source of wonder for visitors who had a chance to observe it. Because most hailed from northern states or Europe, they found the area's fauna positively exotic. As they approached the city by boat, visitors might see numerous species of waterfowl such as ducks, geese, or pelicans, and, before their extinc-

While much has changed along Mobile's riverfront since the antebellum period, the mighty river remains a constant in regional life. This panoramic view of Mobile's port, taken from Cooper Riverside Park, shows the heart of the old harbor as it appears today, the center of a complex featuring a convention center, museum, and cruise terminal. Most of the cargo delivered or loaded aboard ships in port takes place just north and south of this area. Photograph by the author.

The British geologist George William Featherstonhaugh spent several decades of his life in the United States working as a scientist and surveyor. His account of his experiences in the South was published in 1844 as *Excursion through the Slave States*. Courtesy of the Library of Congress.

tion, noisy flocks of diminutive and colorful "paroquets" (*sic*). The naturalist Philip Henry Gosse studied some of the region's wildlife perhaps a little more closely than others. He recorded in his journal how, upon entering Mobile Bay, "flocks of pelicans were flying about," while "shoals of dolphins were wallowing and frisking in the water close to the shore. As we passed within a few hundred yards of the point, many specimens of a pretty moth flew on board; they were Geometrae, with angular wings, of a rich velvety cream colour, without spots. . . . A very fine individual of the black swallowtail butterfly (Papilio Asterius) likewise fluttered about the vessel." Not everyone seemed as entranced by the prolific display of wildlife, though. Numerous gulls followed boats to and from the Gulf, having quickly learned that curious travelers might throw them pieces of bread. Charles Lyell, the Scottish geologist, observed how some men aboard the boat on which he had booked passage took this opportunity to shoot the birds for "mere wantonness."[2]

Even if not everyone appreciated the natural abundance of the area as much as Gosse or Lyell, few could help but be moved by some of the animal behaviors they observed. Several miles north of Mobile along the river, one traveler wrote, "we passed . . . a solitary trunk of a tree, with all its branches gone, standing like a pillar in the wilderness." Atop this trunk, "crowning it like the capital of a column, was an eagle's nest, in which the eagle was then seated." The captain of the steamboat, who had navigated the waterway for more than twenty years, told his passengers that "he remembered the eagle's nest as a landmark used by pilots, when he first came on the river, and he never recollected a single year in which the eagle did not brood over her young there, so that a sort of sanctity was now attached to the tree, which no one seemed disposed to disturb."[3]

The wildly diverse proliferation of plant and tree species in Mobile's subtropical climate transfixed many of Mobile's guests. "The luxuriance and quickness of vegetation here, surprises a northern eye," acknowledged one visitor in a letter sent home in the early 1820s, noting with astonishment that orange and myrtle leaf orange trees, as well as pomegranate and fig trees, seemed to proliferate in and around the city. "Anyone desiring to take a jaunt to the outskirts of the city will feel overwhelmed by the wealth of choices confronting him," exclaimed another. "Everywhere so far as one can see, there is nothing but thick green groves, picturesque rolling country, meadows

The celebrated pianist and composer Henri Herz toured extensively in Europe, South America, and North America during his career. His journals detailing his experiences in the United States, where he conducted a multiyear tour between 1846 and 1850, were published a century later by the State Historical Society of Wisconsin as *My Travels in America*. Courtesy of the Library of Congress.

decked with flowers and carpeted with luxuriant grass, a striking contrast to the swamp and mud holes encountered in the country surrounding the Crescent City of New Orleans."[4]

Indeed the greenery in and about Mobile at all times of year astonished some visitors, who described the area as a sort of garden spot of which they had little knowledge beforehand. "In sailing out into the Gulph of Mexico we passed several islands covered with a most charming vegetation," recalled John Shaw, who took during an extended journey through the South in the 1850s. He wrote of observing innumerable species of "flowers, shrubs, and trees" and noted with rapture how "the shore was covered with the most beautiful white sand, sweetly contrasting with the colour of the water, and the fine exhibition of the vegetable world." The French musician Henri Herz had nothing but praise for the physical environment he found in Mobile, describing the city's setting as presenting "a most enchanting aspect, by virtue of its variety—meadows dotted with flowers, verdant brush country, and pine forests recalling cold Norway in the midst of hot Alabama."[5]

Guests who ventured to the outskirts of town encountered roads flanked by lush vegetation. This stirred them to pen some of the most florid passages in their accounts of visits to the city. The actor Tyrone Power described a journey south of the city as proceeding "through a forest of pine and oak . . . decked by a hundred different shrubs and plants, from the magnificent grandiflora." He remembered this ride in the carriage of his host as a delightful sojourn along "the beautiful forest paths which surround this city. The weather was divine even in winter and flowers of great beauty yet in abundance." Another recalled traveling along a road "the hedges of which were entirely composed of Cherokee roses" and remarked how they appeared "lovely, twining fantastically round every tree and shrub with their rich, snowy blossoms." Yet another visitor, arriving in February, noted with amazement how, even though the magnolias were not in bloom, "the wood violets were out in rich though inodorous luxuriance; the jessamines [jasmines] were unfolding their yellow blossoms, redolent of perfume; and the bay-spice displayed on every side its gorgeous crimson flowers and glossy aromatic leaves."[6]

In similar fashion but with words chosen even more carefully, the noted Swedish author Fredrika Bremer recounted her journey to the bayfront, which involved a trip down "a beautiful promenade through a magnolia forest, along the shore of the Mexican Gulf." Waxing almost philosophical about its splendor, she noted how the magnolia "is not a beautiful, but an extremely poetical tree, and when it shoots forth its snow-white fragrant flowers, it seems to recall some beautiful poem of Lord Byron's." She arrived at a spot that provided a view of the head of the bay and wrote of the peculiar charm of this signature vista: "The air was pleasant. The waves of the Mexican Gulf broke softly and broadly against the shore, with a loud but soothing sound. The woods were silent, fresh, and green. I rested, breathed, enjoyed, in deep harmony with the scene around me." Another visitor to the city who ventured to the same spot recalled his wonder at what he saw on a calm day, using more straightforward prose to describe the beauty he found: "We found the waters of the bay smooth and unrippled, like an extensive lake, the woods coming down everywhere to its edge, and the live oaks and long-leaved pines, with the buck-eye and several other trees just beginning to put forth their young leaves. Mobile and its environs are almost perfectly flat, but it has the peculiar beauty of the prairie."[7]

The overwhelming majority of guests whose reactions to Mobile survive arrived in the fall and spring. As I discuss later in this chapter, this was Mobile's busy trading season, when steamboats were running regularly and all its hotels were open—the city shrank to a fraction of its wintertime size in summer, which brought oppressive heat and humidity and the ever-present threat of yellow fever. Most therefore encountered the Gulf Coast town and environs when their climate was most pleasant, for the region features mild winters with cool nights and warm days and a marked decline in humidity levels for long stretches. Biting insects also are much less prevalent in the cooler seasons. Many praised the weather as ideal as a consequence. Perhaps they would have thought otherwise had they experienced the blanket of oppressive humidity, high temperatures, and almost daily rains, studded with frequent downpours, that characterize summer. But the Mobile they knew proved to be, by and large, the best version of itself imaginable.

"I found this climate the most delightful imaginable," remembered one visitor during a particularly pleasant autumn. "I never felt in England during the summer season such an agreeable temperature and climate as I experienced at Mobile at their coldest season of the year." Aware of how different things might be in a different season, however, he cautioned that "in the summer season it would be certain death for a foreigner to inhale its poisonous atmosphere." One European visitor remarked during a January stay that "the weather was very fine, and as warm as we have it in summer. I felt it very much in walking, and most of the doors and windows in the houses stood open." Others were amazed at the number of warm days they experienced during the winter season and the natural growth of flora that accompanied them: "The thermometer since December, has been several times up to 84, and but once or twice down below 40. The 15th of February, the plumb [sic] and peach trees were in full blossom," according to the *New York Spectator*. Lyell journeyed to the city from Tuscaloosa in February 1846. He remembered with wonder how the temperature in Tuscaloosa was 17 degrees as he prepared to depart for the Gulf Coast, but as he traveled downriver, he saw abundant signs of spring. The closer he came to Mobile and beheld many plants and trees in full bloom, the more distant winter seemed.[8]

Visitors were enchanted by the "indescribable softness in this Southern clime, a delicious indolence in its atmosphere," which at least one writer characterized as nothing less than delicious, containing "the happiest combination of warmth and freshness ... a fine breeze from the sea, and a balmy softness in the atmosphere." Fredrika Bremer, who spent time in the city in January 1851, exclaimed her joy at encountering "perfect midsummer weather" during what for most visitors would have been the coldest time of year back home. She praised the "delicious sensation as [Mobile's climate] occasions." This was also a dry period, and she raved how "that beautiful, beneficent southern sun, shines here all day long."[9]

But one need not be in town during the dog days of July, August, and early September to get a good taste of what midsummer on the Gulf Coast can feel like. Guests who experienced the rising temperatures and oppressive humidity of some early spring days were decidedly less than delighted with the climate than those who arrived at midwinter. "The sun here has a force not to be denied," noted John Oldmixon, a Brit. "Even so early as March I found the growing heat very oppressive. ... There is a kind of clammy, misty, calm heat here in the south" that forced people to "gasp for breath." One visitor who approached Mobile from New Orleans in early summer aboard a stagecoach noted how his party felt the full effects of blazing heat as they neared Mobile:

"The sun shining down upon us like all wrath." He observed that "about 1 o'clock we were overtaken by a sudden and violent shower—filling all the unoccupied space on the stage with water, soaking to saturation the leather-covered cushions, and rendering them cool if not delightful." Another visitor, who had dared to stay in the city until early summer, summarized the sauna-like climate of the region while explaining how locals could survive such intense heat: "Although it is but the eighth day of June, the weather is considered to have reached its utmost degree of heat. Imagine the hottest weather you ever felt, continued for three months without intermission, accompanied by clouds of mosquitoes and armies of fleas, and you will have an idea of our summer." Locals were able to tolerate these conditions with the "aid of the southerly breeze which blows in from the sea and tempers the air."[10]

Few visitors spent much time in the city during the peak of hurricane season, so most would not have felt the fury of the tropical storms that then, as now, threatened Mobile every year. But visitors were nonetheless well aware of hurricanes' ravages. They have long been perhaps the most dreaded aspect of life along the Gulf Coast. Descriptions of storms that swept over the city and left evidence of their fury for months or years afterward provided material for dinner table conversation with those who visited the city in the aftermath. The local socialite Octavia LeVert left a vivid account of a storm's landfall near Mobile in her diary. "Mobile has been visited by the most terrific Hurricane of this Century," she proclaimed. "Oh! The horrors, the terrors of that night no words can shadow forth.... The wind had the sound of Cannon and struck the house, with the force of its Balls. Then would come a wail—like myriads of human voices in their Death Agony.... My soul went up in fervent prayer." With dozens of homes and businesses utterly destroyed, hundreds if not thousands of trees blown down in all directions, the city appeared to her as "one mass of terrible ruin." Few travelers devoted many lines to these events in their published narratives, but the long-standing effects of such events could not have entirely escaped their notice and more than likely helped reinforce the perfect dread they had of staying in Mobile during the warmer months.[11]

Visitors also seemed to marvel at the cold spells that sometimes descend on the region during the winter, apparently under the impression such anomalies were infrequent. Yet, in most winters, Mobile will experience a short blast or two of frigid arctic air that can drive temperatures well below freezing for a day or two. Encountering such weather proved to be a novel experience for guests in the city. "Now you must know that the weather has been bitterly cold," observed Margaret Hall in a letter she wrote during her travels along the Gulf Coast in the late 1820s. "The deck of the boat yesterday morning was covered with ice." A traveler who kept detailed records of daily temperatures during his visit noted during one period in February when the thermometer stood at 22 degrees at sunrise and had climbed to only 30 at noon. An account of a day in Mobile during an exceptionally cold period in 1852 appeared in the *New York Times;* it noted how Mobile Bay lay partially frozen during one of the fiercest blasts of northern air the city had ever seen. "Skates have been in demand—the like was never heard of before in Mobile," the writer proclaimed. Such weather is indeed atypical during Mobile winters, but even in the colder spells guests found something enervating in the Gulf Coast climate. One visitor in late December found that "there is frost, but not hard frost, the sun [is] bright and the sky clear as crystal; in fact, splendid weather."[12]

The greenery of the gardens flanking Mobile's streets, studding its yards, and in evidence all around the city and its environs captured the attention of many travelers as one of the city's most distinguishing features. "In the gardens at Mobile," noted one charmed pedestrian, "there were jonquils and snowdrops in flower, and ... we saw that beautiful evergreen, the yellow jessamine, in full bloom." Frederick Law Olmsted, a man who certainly knew his way around a garden, stood enchanted by the flowers and fruit-bearing plants he found growing with ease in Mobile. "Figs are abundant, and bananas and oranges are said to be grown with some care, and slight winter protection," he recorded. Other travelers noted numerous stands of the Cherokee rose hedge, which "climbs over everything and covers the trees with its rich foliage and flowers." Visitors traversed with delight streets that at least one person described as "quite delicious" and for good reason, given the profusion of ornamental shrubs and fruit trees such as peach and orange. Another traveler described being taken on a "pretty drive" around the city and getting a chance to see a unique "nursery-garden" in which the proprietor had grown a cactus with hanging roots. The city, according to some, was nothing less than "a cluster of gardens," each with some particular attraction worthy of notice.[13]

Frederick Law Olmsted, regarded as the father of landscape architecture in America, is perhaps best remembered for designing New York's Central Park. Olmsted enjoyed a successful career as a journalist as well. The *New York Daily Times* commissioned him to undertake an extensive tour of the southern United States in the 1850s that resulted in the publication of three acclaimed volumes. His time in Mobile is recounted in *A Journey in the Seaboard Slave States, with Remarks on Their Economy* (1856). Courtesy of the Library of Congress.

The city's trees drew the most attention from observers, however. At Mobile visitors beheld tree species "growing to the very edge of the sea, interspersed with equally magnificent pines and evergreen oaks." They noted the "profusion of shade-trees and shrubbery" along the city's streets, remarking especially on the "immense live oaks, stretching out their giant arms a hundred feet." Another observer enthralled by the city's variety of trees noted, "The environs of Mobile are charming. Few houses are without the greatest variety of shade trees. Orange trees abound; but the live oak everywhere rears its majestic Alp of foliage, casting beneath shade broad enough to shelter from the sun a herd of cattle. . . . There are superb groups of them in and about this city. They shade the lawns and give dignity to the mansions that lift their roofs above them." Some took note of the numerous Pride of India trees planted along city streets; the ornamental species, which is similar in appearance to a crepe myrtle, was popular in urban areas at the time. In addition to a brilliant display of flowers, its blooms, according to witnesses, were good for "filling the air with fragrance." One unimpressed visitor sniffed, "As a city Mobile offers few attractions to the traveler, and only one street [Government Street] which has any pretensions to beauty." Those pretensions were, in his estimation, "deliverable more from its width, and the luxuriant tropical beauty of the trees which shade it on either side, than from its architecture."[14]

Save for the Greek and Italian Renaissance Revival homes of the wealthy that began to pop up along Mobile's streets in the late 1850s, and a few similarly designed public buildings, visitors found little noteworthy in the city's built environment. At least in part this is attributable to the relatively small size of the town in its first few decades and the haphazard nature of private and public construction at the time. In 1822, for example, the city had just 240 frame houses, and the complete inventory of its public structures consisted of a bank, a post office and customhouse, a courthouse and jail, two churches, three bakeries, several dozen stores of all varieties, and a series of wharves along the riverfront. The core of the city extended for about a mile along the river and approximately the same distance away from it. Commerce and Royal were the main business streets; just to the northwest and southwest, including Congress, Monroe, St. Anthony, and Lawrence Streets, were some of the primary residential areas. The great majority of these homes in the 1810s and 1820s were single-story cottages that evoked colonial or Federal styles and revealed the European, vernacular, and early American influences that mirrored much of the city's population at the time. By any estimation, the city's public architecture in the first decades of the antebellum era could be described as unimpressive. A jail appears to have been the first public building erected by city officials, and the town had no courthouse until the 1820s—a simple rectangular structure. Fire consumed the courthouse just a few years after its construction, and its brick replacement on the corner of Government and Royal Streets went up in flames in 1828. The latter building is believed to have featured one of the first columned porticos in Alabama. The city's first public market opened in the early 1820s, and a few small and unornamented government-owned facilities, such as a powder house, were erected that decade. Most of these structures were wooden and less durable than those that would be built in the city in later years.[15]

At least in its early American period, the city also exhibited little in the way of an urban plan. The private business interests spurring the city's expansion had a rather free hand in crafting its built environment. In a time of little government regulation of any sort, this meant a virtual free-for-all that resulted in a rapidly changing community with almost no discernible order to its growth. The venerable but decrepit old Fort Carlota (Fort Charlotte to the British and Fort Conde to the French), the landmark defensive post around which colonial Mobile had taken shape, was deemed unnecessary and unworthy of repair shortly after the American government took over the city by and hastily had the fort demolished. The resulting tons of debris became fill for marshy areas near riverfront streets, and new streets were run through the area the fort had occupied. The resulting "compactly built, dirty, and noisy" business district, in the words of at least one visitor, contained "little elegance, or evidence of taste or public spirit." Dozens of new wharves of varying size and design went up in haphazard fashion along the riverfront as lot owners sought to take best advantage of their waterfront real estate, and trading houses of every description soon popped up along an expanding grid of dirt streets.[16]

With its hodgepodge of architectural styles, little to no zoning of any type, inadequate drainage of its primitive streets, and a crude sewerage system that essentially emptied open ditches directly into the river, the Mobile of the early antebellum period appeared to be a coarse frontier town with little to recommend it architecturally. Because the business of the port occupied so much of its focus, many early visitors found Mobile to be an unornamented working town. "The portion of the town immediately contiguous to the quays," remembered one visitor in a typical assessment, "is about as unattractive as the corresponding parts of most seaport towns are found to be."[17]

Especially in its early years but throughout the antebellum period, visitors had reason to suspect that Mobile's metamorphosis from frontier backwater to contemporary metropolis would be gradual. "I have often seen in print and heard the remark that Mobile is a 'one horse town,'" quipped one resident in a local paper who went on to point out that "a stranger coming here would certainly say that the appellation was not merited. He would meet in every street of our rural city not only 'one horse,' but several horses, running at large ... [plus] our other domestic animals, such as cows, goats, and pigs, and the numberless curs." Loose livestock and stray dogs were a constant nuisance in the city in this period. Travelers did make occasional comments about the numerous quadrupeds allowed to roam Mobile's streets, and at least two pointed out one of the most disagreeable consequences. "I was surprised to observe dead horses and cows suffered to lie exposed on the [river's] shore, scarce out of town," remembered one tourist. Another went further, describing how the numerous carcasses of horses, cows, and mules along the riverfront attracted packs of wild dogs. To John Oldmixon it seemed the community stood helpless to deal with the situation because, he had observed, "everybody complains," but "nobody cares; nobody will obey anybody, or observe any sort of regulation, no matter how good or essential."[18]

Gradually, however, touches of urban refinement began to appear in the landscape as the city grew in population and economic influence. Beginning in the 1830s, the pace of growth became truly phenomenal. "In every direction the eye meets buildings going up and other improvements progressing," reported one visitor in 1835, who stated that at least fifty new stores and a hundred new homes had been built within the last year. Such expansion was impressive enough on its own, but the frequent fires that swept the city in its early American years provided impetus for more new construction than might have been expected otherwise. In general, once a fire ravaged a swath of the old city, it was rebuilt bigger and better as the era progressed; Mobile had entered "a phase of prosperity and growth that permitted men to conceive of the monumental," according to the architectural historian Elizabeth Barrett Gould.[19]

By about 1840, the rough-edged trading town was becoming a showplace for the Classical Revival architecture then in vogue in America. Domestic, religious, and civic structures constructed during the rapid and unprecedented growth from the 1830s to the 1850s frequently featured Greek Revival designs, for example. Those completed just before the Civil War by talented designers and craftsman builders, working in the most popular styles and exhibiting exacting detail, left the unmistakable impression of a city "on the make."[20]

A massive city hospital, a growing number of blocks of adjoined brick commercial structures, and a number of well-appointed hotels, banks, and churches completely recast the city from a sleepy colonial backwater into a thriving and modern metropolis in just a few decades. The number, size, and craftsmanship of the homes of Mobile's wealthiest citizens especially caught visitors' eyes and elicited the most comment about the city's architecture. Planned beautification efforts in the late antebellum period, such as the landscaping of public squares, also lent an air of sophistication and grace to the erstwhile rough-and-tumble trading town. In the late 1850s, for example, city officials decorated Bienville Square with iron fencing, added curbing and sidewalks, and improved Washington Square in similar fashion. A visitor to the town in the 1820s would have read with disbelief the opinion of George Featherstonhaugh, who in 1844 published an account of his journey through the city, writing, "At every step I took I was more and more struck with the universal love of order, and the good taste which seemed to prevail."[21]

To experience the city, though, travelers had to negotiate a growing network of streets of uneven quality whose shortcomings became one of the most commented-upon subjects in accounts of Mobile. Depending on when during the period they visited and the weather conditions during their trip, opinions of the quality of the city's thoroughfares and the ease of transportation along them varied wildly. One visitor account from the 1820s, when the city was very much on the make but still a backwater town, remarked about watching as streets beyond the commercial center were carved from the wilderness. Tyrone Power took a carriage ride from the riverfront during a stay in town for a series of performances during a hectic period of the city's early growth and remembered roads "cleared by the woodsman's axes; the stumps were not as yet macadamized by time, still the horses picked their way amongst them at a very fair pace." He found "broad streets already marked out: plunging deep into the forest, many scattered houses of brick were springing up on sites where barely trees enough had been cut down to afford elbow-room for the builders." Another guest at about the same time noted how "every street in Mobile terminates either at the river or in the wild forest," a succinct picture of a community undergoing rapid expansion as its infrastructure struggled to keep pace.[22]

Gradually, though, starting with the streets of Mobile's central business district and extending to the more prosperous residential areas of town, the streets would be improved and covered with crushed oyster shell as a sort of pavement. This locally abundant material became a hallmark of the city's built environment, in fact, with most visitor accounts making some reference to the paving found only in coastal communities at the time. "The main streets are long and broad, well shaded by trees," noted one traveler in the 1840s, "and admirably paved." The particularly scenic bayside road leading south of the city to Choctaw Point became one of the most mentioned

The Bay Shell Road, which ran south of Mobile alongside the upper reaches of the bay, became a favorite local attraction in the antebellum era. It would remain so for decades. These views, a print that appeared in an 1850s edition of *Harper's Weekly* and a photograph taken circa 1900, provide glimpses of this lost roadway. Courtesy of the Library of Congress.

aspects of the city's infrastructure; the passageway through immense waterside growths of magnolia and live oak was paved with oyster shell. George Featherstonhaugh, the British scientist who also visited in the 1840s, could not help but praise the urban grid he beheld, roadways well laid out "at right angles, with excellent sidewalks, the streets between them being graduated and macadamized with the sea-shells that are found in the greatest abundance." Taken together, he pronounced Mobile's streets the "most solid and the cleanest streets I ever have seen in any country."[23]

However, only a minority of visitors would have agreed with him during the pre–Civil War years. Many of those who left published accounts of antebellum Mobile decried the city's streets as little better than muddy ditches, at least in wet weather. Considering the Gulf Coast is among the rainiest sections of the country, that meant most of the time. "Mobile is, with the exception of Quebec," complained one visitor in the 1850s, "decidedly the muddiest town I ever saw; even to get from the hotel to the steamer, a distance of some few hundred yards, we were forced to hire a carriage, for fear of being mired." Bishop Henry Benjamin Whipple, on a journey through the South in the 1830s, would have seconded this soggy assessment. As he explained to his readers, "The land about Mobile is very low, and much of it is exceedingly swampy. . . . Much of the business part of the city is made land and during the rainy season the streets are nearly impassable on account of the mud. At such times the streets resemble miry stage roads more than the pavements of the city." In truth, the drainage ditches that flanked some downtown streets, bordered in places by logs, became little more than holding ponds in wet weather. Tales persist that the local alligators once inhabited them— perhaps an exaggerated claim but not far-fetched.[24]

Even in drier weather, the frequent deluges left washes and ruts that made the streets difficult to navigate. "The streets are not paved, and unpleasant from the depth of sand," one visitor noted. Whipple found the environmental transition he experienced in Mobile to be so sudden "that one is either wading in mud or suffocating with dust," and he pronounced the city's streets "worse than any I have ever seen." Another bemoaned the "sandy streets of Mobile . . . cut up into ten thousand shifting, harmless ruts." Other travelers found the roads beyond the city center were often rather primitive. Duke Karl Bernhard of Germany, touring the town in the late 1820s, vividly described the perimeter thoroughfares as bordered by woods on one side and "ditches and marshes" on the other, forcing him to limit his travels to the principal streets of the main business corridor. Though few travelers mention it, simply getting from place to place by city streets must have been difficult in any circumstance: as late as the 1850s only a few street names were posted on corners and only a few buildings had address numbers on them.[25]

The one street that drew the most notice from the city's guests—and perhaps needed little identifying signage—was Government Street. The thoroughfare extended westward from the riverfront through the heart of the business district and continued for more than two miles into the pine and oak forests surrounding the city; as the antebellum era progressed, the street became a popular location to build a residence. A sort of grand promenade boasting some of the largest homes in the city, the street was more than a hundred feet wide as it cut through the city center, making it by far Mobile's widest and a natural showcase for its emerging built environment. "A broad, straight alley of beautiful villas, surrounded by trees and garden-plots" is how one visitor remembered the road, while another remembered it as a broad thoroughfare "finished in a very admirable style."[26]

Guests were enchanted with what they beheld along its length. Amelia M. Murray, visiting in the 1850s, pronounced Government Street nothing less than "the handsomest street I have seen anywhere; it consists of detached

Today, Arlington Park Pier, located south of downtown adjacent to industrial complexes, is one of the few publicly accessible waterside spots near the route of the old Bay Shell Road. Visitors can still see stunning views of the bay and the mouth of the Mobile River, as well as a constant stream of vessels entering and leaving the port. Photograph by the author.

houses with gardens; some have the usual fault in this country of being whitened to a dazzling and unnatural whiteness; but a custom-house is in process of erection, with granite of a soft grey colour, and it seems likely to be an example of good architecture, as well as of a pleasing tint." James Silk Buckingham, a British journalist, likewise believed the street was "as handsome an avenue as is to be seen in the country . . . lined with rows of trees on either hand, protected by an excellent flag-pavement at the sides, and already ornamented with some exceedingly handsome public structures, and private mansions and dwellings." Yet another visitor declared Government Street the only "handsome street" in the town but drew particular attention to its "houses . . . built in the English style, with abundance of shrubs in the gardens."[27]

The numerous massive homes built in classical styles with wide porches facing the smooth, wide road stood out as a unique section of the city that drew much comment from visitors. One guest believed he detected a harmony in the scale of Government Street homes and proclaimed that "the buildings, too, are appropriate to the beauty and width of the street, some of them being stately structures of brick." The American writer Joseph Holt Ingraham declared it "one of the finest streets I have ever seen. It is a broad, smooth, almost imperial avenue, lined chiefly by the abodes of the 'merchant nobles.'"[28]

Built in 1855 by Judge John Bragg, brother of the Confederate general Braxton Bragg, the Bragg-Mitchell Mansion is one of the few remaining grand estates in the Mobile area. Courtesy of the Library of Congress.

Indeed, the largest, most elaborate homes in the city belonged to the wealthy businessmen whose fortunes derived from the cotton trade. In truth, only a few homes in Mobile were the columned, multistory mansions built in the revival styles we have come to associate with the wealth of the southern aristocracy during the antebellum era. Yet the mystique surrounding them has made them so evocative of a particular time and place that people think they were much more common than they actually were. Even today, cities with a rich antebellum heritage such as Mobile's still highlight those relative few that remain as some of their most iconic architectural specimens. But enough examples of these edifices were built that the stereotypical image of the Old South has some basis in fact. Mobile was a place where large amounts of money could be made from cotton, the South's most valuable commodity. And the fine homes that wealth paid for were concentrated along the principal residential streets a short distance from the city center and therefore were visible to visitors. Guests taken aback by the scale and detail of the architecture of these homes and their other appointments could not help but comment on the spectacle.[29]

"Some of the merchants here live magnificently—their houses are really mansions; a great many have handsome equipages," Oldmixon observed during his stay in the early 1850s. "Columns, porticos, rich cornices, handsome verandahs meet the eye everywhere." He concluded that Mobile "is a city of villas, the upper part standing in their own small gardens." Another writer, similarly smitten with the grounds of Mobile's manses as much as their architectural detail, noted that "a great many homes . . . looked attractive . . . with front yards and shrubbery and flowers." The "almost universality of open verandas, beneath which the inhabitants were sitting to enjoy the cool breath of evening" drew the praise of another. Yet another seconded the observation, noting that "almost all [of Mobile's nicer homes] are surrounded by verandas and gardens filled with roses, orange and lemon trees, and magnificent magnolias." Featherstonhaugh, never at a loss for words, acknowledged having difficulty finding the right words to describe the pleasing scene he beheld in the city's more posh neighborhoods, where he saw "numerous houses built of wood, neatly painted white, with large plots of land attached to them, fenced in with painted palings." Another visitor declared, "The view up the long, shaded, garden streets lined with white villas, with their green blinds, is enchanting."[30]

Those familiar with the architectural history of the South know that most of these striking villas were built in the last two decades before the Civil War. The 1840s and 1850s are recognized as the height of the Classical Revival movement in the region, and most of the stunning two-story columned homes of the city's wealthiest residents were built during that period. But what, if anything, in the way of domestic architecture did guests in earlier decades observe and remark upon? The answer is very little, if the number of comments in published accounts is any indication. Numerous cottage-style homes, some of them wood and masonry, would have populated city streets at the beginning of the American period. The overwhelming majority were simple wood structures. A few intriguing references to the visible reminders of the city's long colonial history appear in the extant literature, such as that provided by Karl Bernhard, the German duke, during a stay in Mobile in the 1820s. He noted seeing "some Spanish houses which consist of timber frames, of which the open spaces are filled up with beaten clay [a type of stucco]" in what we now recognize was a transitional period as the city emerged as a dynamic trading center early in the American era. But such appraisals are few, leaving the unmistakable impression that whatever early visitors observed, they deemed it unexceptional. Even as late as the 1840s, visitors such as Henri Herz were moved to describe Mobile as "not distinguished for its public edifices, but its homes are comfortable."[31]

Just a few years later, however, those who ventured to the city, such as William Tecumseh Sherman, on duty in the Mobile area before the Civil War, were leaving enchanting and detailed descriptions of the well-appointed homes and spacious lots of the city's wealthier residents. Sherman wrote,

> On the river [Mobile] resembles any other business city but as you leave the wharves and go back you find beautiful streets . . . ornamented with trees and in front of the houses a little garden bed now and then shows a profusion of roses and shrubs—a little further and they begin to assume a beauty, neatness and comfort I never elsewhere beheld. The houses are mostly white with piazzas all around with all kinds of roses and flowers creeping up the latticed portico. They are generally situated about one or two hundred yards back from the road, or rather street, with a carriage road to the very door passing under an arbor of shade trees. In all other respects each exercises his own taste and judgement, and thereby have created for Mobile the most beautiful suburbs and country seats in this country.

Others, including the writer Emmeline Stuart Wortley, Olmsted, and Ingraham, similarly remarked on the proliferation of beautiful villas and scenic gardens in and around the city. Collectively, they left visitors in the late antebellum period with the impression that Mobile was "an opulent place."[32]

CHAPTER 4

A Place for Business

*The wharves for a mile are piled with cotton bales.
The very trees are draped and made ugly by its flying about.*
—*John Oldmixon*

One need only to stroll briefly through its main thoroughfares and especially along its wharves in order to observe there the extraordinary business activity evident on all sides.
—*Charles Olliffe*

The defining characteristic of antebellum Mobile in the eyes of visitors lay in its role as a center of business, and for good reason. A "flourishing seaport" by the mid-nineteenth century as one of the city's premier historians, John Sledge, has put it, Mobile became the epicenter of a regional trading network centered on the exportation of cotton to world markets, the staggering scale of which stunned and intrigued the city's guests. Regardless of their length of stay in town or the purpose of their visit, travelers who wrote any description of Mobile almost invariably described it first and foremost as a booming trading port with a remarkable focus on a single article of commerce. The New England journalist Hiram Fuller provided a summary assessment of Mobile at the height of its commercial activity in the 1850s that anyone visiting the place at the time would have recognized and has often been reprinted in histories of the community. He described the place sarcastically as "a pleasant cotton city of some thirty thousand inhabitants—where the people live in cotton houses and ride in cotton carriages. They buy cotton, sell cotton, think cotton, eat cotton, drink cotton, and dream cotton. They marry cotton wives, and unto them are born cotton children. In enumerating the charms of a fair widow, they begin by saying she makes so many bales of cotton. It is the great staple—the sum and substance of Alabama. It has made Mobile, and all its citizens."[1]

Even early in the nineteenth century, before Mobile's commercial maturity as one of the Gulf region's most vibrant ports, visitors recognized the

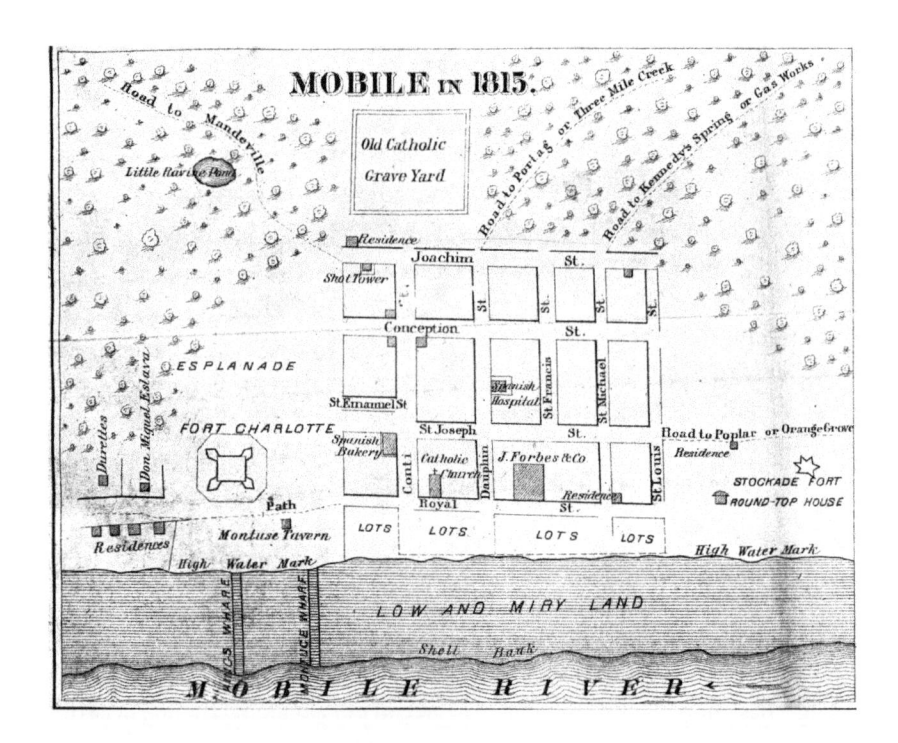

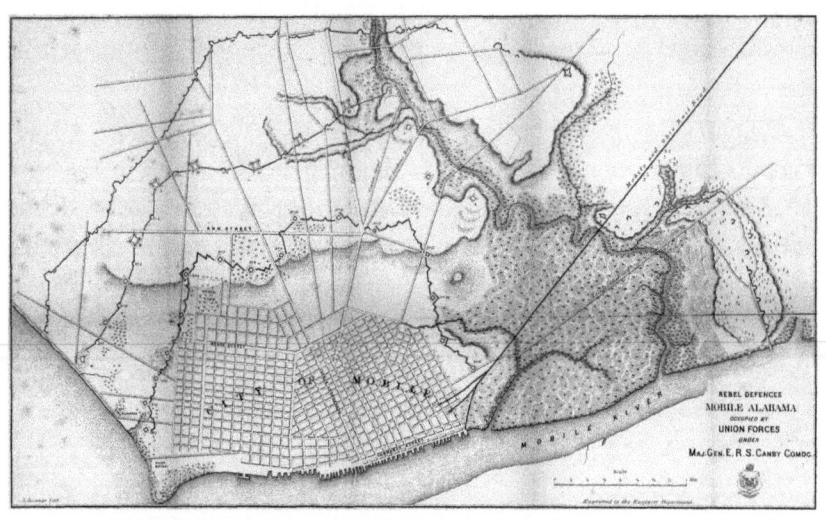

These maps of Mobile, produced in 1815 and 1865, show the dramatic growth of the city's various docks, wharves, and piers during a half century of development. The 1865 map also shows the defensive earthworks constructed around the perimeter of the city during the Civil War. Top: courtesy of the Historic Mobile Preservation Society. Bottom: courtesy of the Library of Congress.

unmistakable advantages it held for trade and predicted its inevitable rise. "This must become a considerable place for export and import, when once better known to the mercantile world," one visitor predicted in 1816, just a few years after its acquisition by the United States. Several guests of the city in those early American years raved about its possibilities in remarkably similar language, proclaiming the city to be "advantageously situated for commerce," having a "most advantageous situation," or a location "advantageous for commerce." In the words of one visitor to Mobile in 1817, the city could not help but soon "become a place of much trade," given its unique location at the head of a spacious bay at the mouth of one of the largest river systems in southeastern North America.[2]

The realization of such rich promise would come in relatively short order, for by the late 1820s the city had already become well established as a hub for regional trade and seemed to have found its calling. "The maritime position of Mobile, with one foot upon the Gulf, and one hand grasping a quiver of rivers... determines its commercial character," wrote one person who arrived just before the Civil War. Others had expressed similar opinions of the town's robust business activity, which, despite periodic fluctuations, made Mobile's trading volume by far Alabama's largest throughout the pre–Civil War period. Early in the era, the city became a regional "commercial emporium," especially for cotton, and the "great mart [for many goods from] ... all the country on the Gulf east of the Mississippi." Mobile would only grow in this regard throughout the period. By the 1850s visitors unhesitatingly referred to Mobile as the "principal outlet of the commerce of the State of Alabama," and "as a depot for all the good things of this bountiful land." Descriptions of the trading activity witnessed by visitors pepper the published accounts, ranging from understated estimations of the city as a cotton port to one that enthused that Mobile was "one of the most important of American cities ... rapidly increasing its population and its trade." All agreed that Mobile was a place on the rise.[3]

Despite all its natural advantages, the city had faced a serious but short-lived challenge from the town of Blakeley in the 1820s (see chapter 2). The project was the brainchild of a local planter, Josiah Blakeley, who hailed from the Northeast with a background in public service. He had helped arrange for the charter of Mobile as a U.S. city but believed the tangle of waterways emptying into Mobile Bay provided more than enough room for two trading cities. He planned the town that bore his name on a bluff along the deep and wide Tensaw River opposite Mobile in 1814. The site had some features that Mobile did not: a site along a high and dry bluff with a good supply of freshwater and beside a navigable river that connected to the same river system that was servicing the old colonial city of Mobile. Although Blakeley died before he could see his dreams become a reality, the city he founded had become a veritable boom town by the early 1820s and, for a few years, worked with vigor to siphon off from Mobile much of the maritime trade in cotton and lumber entering the delta from the Alabama and Tombigbee River systems.[4]

Visitors to the area in the 1820s and early 1830s were struck by this simmering local trading war between cities "contending vehemently for the privilege of becoming that great emporium . . . for the produce of the young fertile State of Alabama." Blakeley stood as "an elegant and pleasant spot," according to an early travel guide, which also gushed that it was "well situated for commerce." It went on to note that "vessels drawing eleven feet [of] water can enter the port at full tide" and pointed out that "the same wind that enables a vessel to enter Mobile Bay will carry her to the wharves of Blakeley." Blakeley's boom had become a bust by 1830, however, as epidemics of yellow fever, rising land prices, and rapidly expanding facilities in Mobile and navigational improvements to its harbor so checked the progress of its erstwhile rival that Mobile became the lone major trading community in the region. It would not look back.[5]

By the 1830s Mobile's riverside wharves, cotton warehouses, and other portside facilities throbbed with trade. The spectacle of the port in full swing drew visitors to remark on its novelty. Judging from their enchantment, it may have been the city's paramount attraction. "The harbor was a busy scene of commerce and action, crowded with vessels and ships of every possible description," noted a visitor from Ohio named John Morris. He was especially captivated by the city's commercial vibrancy, writing that "lying at the wharves, either loading or unloading, crowded with cotton and other merchandise, were scores of river steamers, lake steamers, coasting vessels, and various sorts of smaller water-craft." Visitors at the height of the winter cotton trading season were frequently treated to the novel sight of dozens of ships crowding the city's port facilities while loading cotton or waiting in line to do so. "Along the shore is a wooden quay, and wooden piers or landing bridges project into the water, for the convenience of vessels," observed the German duke Karl Bernhard, who counted more than thirty ships lining the docks. A French visitor named Charles Olliffe recalled that the level of bustle at the city's port and in its primary commercial streets nearby surprised him. He passed on to readers of his travel journal that they would "need only to stroll briefly through its main thoroughfares and especially along its wharves in order to observe there the extraordinary business activity evident on all sides."[6]

That business activity was enormous. Some visitors recorded the volume of trade in raw numbers in their narratives, astounded at their size and believing them to be perhaps the best illustration of what they had witnessed. In her book, the British sociologist Harriet Martineau gave detailed dollar amounts to communicate the size of Mobile's shipping business in the 1830s, providing tables that read more like a port authority's economic impact report than a typical travel narrative. She noted that in 1830 the value of imports received at the city's port was estimated at more than $143,000 (more than $4.7 million in 2023) and that in 1834 that figure had risen to nearly $400,000 ($14.2 million in 2023). The city's exports, however, were valued at nearly $2 million ($66.7 million in 2023) and approximately $6 million ($214.2 million in 2023), respectively. Other tourist-authors included in their account a few such figures they obtained while in town to illustrate Mobile's economic vitality. That travelers staying in town for only a few days had easy access to such figures reveals both their fascination with them and the statistics' centrality to Mobile's day-to-day life. The value and volume of the cotton trade offered a good reflection of Mobile's economic health. Historians who have studied Mobile's antebellum cotton trade have determined that the fiber comprised as much as 99 percent of the goods exported from the port in any given year, as cotton became the single driving force of the city's economy and the lone commercial activity around which everything in the city seemed to turn.[7]

By any measure, the phenomenal growth in Mobile's cotton exports during the antebellum decades is noteworthy and defined the city's economic trajectory until the Civil War. In 1818 the city sent a relatively paltry 7,000 bales to world markets, but by the winter of 1858–59 it sent more than

Three-panel sketch of the Government Street Wharf in 1828. Courtesy of the Historic Mobile Preservation Society.

500,000 bales to domestic and international ports. The entire U.S. cotton crop in the late 1850s averaged 2 million to 2.5 million bales. As early as the 1830s Mobile's port had surpassed Savannah and Charleston as a center for cotton exportation. Only New Orleans would export more cotton in the two decades before the Civil War. By 1860 Mobile's cotton trade was valued at about $40 million (nearly $1.5 billion in 2023), making it one of the top ports in the nation in terms of export value. The city fully embraced the trade: the original city seal depicted a ship with a cotton bale above it and the motto AGRICULTURE AND COMMERCE below.[8]

Roughly half of Mobile's cotton exports was shipped to British ports, with ports in the northeastern United States receiving the next largest share; French ports received a smaller but sizable portion as well. This gave Mobile a certain amount of recognition in the many corners of the world affected by the international cotton trade, and several European visitors to the city during the antebellum period either arrived well aware of the city's transatlantic commercial connections or became intrigued by them. The Scottish writer Thomas Hamilton introduced his account of a short stay in Mobile by summarizing it as "a town, as every Liverpool merchant well knows, of considerable importance." The Scottish journalist Charles Mackay observed that "Mobile and Liverpool are ... as closely connected by interest and business as Liverpool and Manchester." The naturalist Phillip Henry Gosse noted during his visit that "a flourishing trade exists in cotton, the staple of the State, with Liverpool, London, Havre, and the ports of the northern United States." The British presence in Mobile would have been hard to miss; so many representatives of British firms had their offices on one short street near the river that some locals referred to it, tongue-in-cheek, as the "English Channel."[9]

While numerous northern and foreign firms played important roles in Mobile's cotton trade, the antebellum city had its closest economic relationship with New York City. Already America's economic colossus by the early nineteenth century, New York became the point to and from which a large portion of Mobile's cotton shipments sailed, and a majority of the brokers and other middlemen operating in the city had direct contact with New York for credit, capital, and access to markets. New York was also the place from which an inordinate share of Mobile's imports were sent—everything from home furnishings and clothing to flour and whiskey. In truth, Mobile

A steamboat loaded with cotton at a dock along the Mobile River in the 1850s. Courtesy of the Alabama Department of Archives and History.

remained in what one of its most prominent historians has bluntly termed a "colonial relationship" with New York and other northern ports throughout the pre–Civil War era. While Mobile hosted the various facilities and provided a home for the many representatives of the diverse array of enterprises that arranged for the cotton trade, most of these businesses were headquartered in New York and European trading centers and not locally owned.[10]

The volume of Mobile's imports from New York in the late antebellum years was such that it often proved less costly to order items directly from New York than to have them produced locally. Frederick Law Olmsted, who recorded a conversation he had with a local citizen in Mobile during his stay in the 1850s, illustrated this point rather bluntly. The man said that he "found it cheaper to have all his furniture and clothing made for him, in New York, to order . . . and sent by on express, than to get it in Mobile." Olmsted himself drove the point home by writing about looking for a hat in Mobile after losing one earlier in his trip. He was astonished that he could not find a hatter in the city "though it boasts a population of thirty thousand souls." Locals customarily ordered such goods from elsewhere.[11]

The infrastructure supporting the cotton trade became a hallmark of Mobile's built environment, distinguishing it from any other city in Alabama and most in the Gulf Coast region. The city's system of wharves along the riverfront, many of which sat atop reclaimed land that had originally been streamside marsh, became the epicenter of trading activity. Dirt, bricks, and logs transformed this swampy area into a bustling and expansive docking facility. By the early 1850s about four dozen wharves lined the city's waterfront from One Mile Creek in the north down to Government Street in the south. Collectively, these facilities could at any one time manage more than 40,000 bales of cotton. At the same time, nearby were more than forty massive warehouses that collectively could house well more than 300,000 bales of cotton until they could be loaded into the holds of ships at the wharves. In addition, numerous presses were available to reduce the bales to a third of their normal size so that they would take up less space in the limited interiors of cargo holds. In 1855 the waterfront had eight such steam-powered facilities that collectively were capable of pressing nearly a thousand bales a day.[12]

These structures would have been a key part of the urban skyline that greeted visitors as they approached Mobile aboard steamers and gave them the first hint of the commercial character of the town. This is to say nothing of the numerous offices along downtown streets that employed an assortment of individuals in the inner workings of the cotton economy—brokers who sold the crop on behalf of planters, commission merchants who purchased supplies for the planters to produce a new crop, insurance agents who processed the paperwork and collected fees on policies protecting the investment in the cargo on its voyage, and bankers who played a critical role in supplying the credit necessary for the whole enterprise. Buyers in northeastern U.S. or European ports could wait months or longer to receive the Alabama cotton that had arrived in Mobile.[13]

"Near the port there is a continual bustle, all buildings in this part consisting exclusively of stores, warehouses, and offices, in front of which stand pyramids of cotton-bales," one visitor reported. Even Mobile's hotels, theaters, and restaurants were inextricably tied to the seasonal cotton trade. Without the businessmen and their families that the trade brought to town, many would simply have ceased to exist. One visitor, James A. Davidson, summed up Mobile's commercial activity with a simple assessment that other travelers would have no doubt agreed with: "There is a great deal of business down here."[14]

Visitors could be excused if they came away with the impression that trading cotton was not only Mobile's primary economic activity but perhaps its sole reason for existence. Many, such as Charles Mackay, believed it no exaggeration to say that the city's whole population "either directly or indirectly, live and thrive by the cotton trade." Picking their way through narrow riverside streets lined with, and sometimes almost completely blocked by, cotton or observing the bustle of activity along the wharves, where dozens of workers were constantly manhandling the precious cargo into ships' holds, visitors to Mobile would have found themselves immersed in a cotton world. So omnipresent was cotton in the city's business district during the fall and winter that it sometimes seemed to literally fall from the sky. "The gutters, when it rains (and the rains of Mobile are floods)," Mackay related, "bear down waifs and strays of cotton to the river, and the river is studded and flecked with cotton-drift floating about on its surface like so many nautili." Another visitor observed: "The wharves for a mile are piled with cotton bales. The very trees are draped and made ugly by its flying about."[15]

Other physical reminders of the city's preoccupation with cotton lay everywhere, none more striking than the dozens of workers at the docks whom one writer described almost poetically as "straining every nerve upon the quay . . . loading and unloading ships beneath the full blaze of the sun, on the glassy waters of the bay." The description expresses in somewhat romantic language the brutal reality of the hot, hard, physical work involved in squeezing cotton bales, each weighing several hundred pounds, into the cramped and stuffy holds of ships. The "good display of shipping at the wharves," featuring "a fine view of steamers, taking in and discharging cotton, the great staple—the mighty pivot upon which the business of this city of 30,000 inhabitants revolves," one visitor wrote, became both a tourism attraction and a defining image of the place.[16]

Indeed, many visitors perceived that every other commercial aspect of

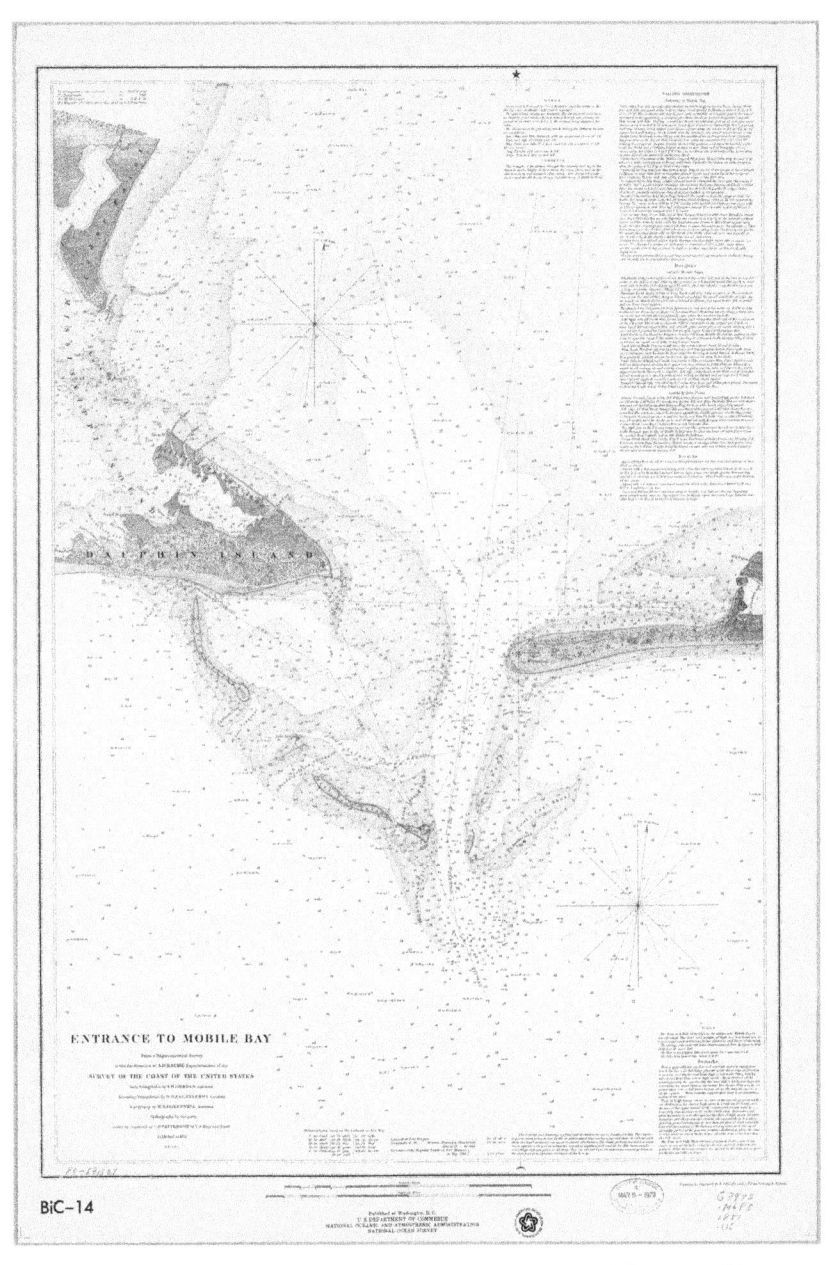

Chart of Lower Mobile Bay, where the "lower fleet" once anchored. Courtesy of the Library of Congress.

Mobile was incidental to cotton. "Mobile is a place of trade, and of nothing else," one visitor remembered. "It is the great port of the cotton-growing State of Alabama." Another wrote, "The cotton trade loomed as the overriding commercial pursuit," struck, as were so many, by the centrality of the fiber to every aspect of life in the town. "Cotton culture and the population grow at the same rate" in Mobile, yet another visitor noted, pointedly summarizing the interconnectedness of the cotton trade and the city's development that other guests expressed in various forms. "The thoughts of the merchants of Mobile are of cotton. They talk of cotton by day, and dream of it by night." In the estimation of the writer Joseph Holt Ingraham, cotton ranked as nothing less than "the circulating blood that gives life to the city. All its citizens are interested in this staple. . . . A failure in a crop of cotton, would cast a cloud over every brow in this city." Even the travel guides that many of the city's guests might have consulted in planning their trips to the region touted the city's commercial character as its defining element. The *Traveller's Guide*, published in 1823, informed readers: "Since the rapid progress of the settlements on the Tombigbee and Alabama [Rivers], Mobile has increased in size and importance. . . . A fireproof warehouse has lately been erected capable of containing 8,000 bales of cotton and provided with presses for re-pressing cotton. A steam-boat plies regularly between Mobile and Tuscaloosa; and another ascends the Alabama to Montgomery."[17]

Some visitors even attempted to explain what, in their estimation, Mobile lacked because of how intensely it focused on the cotton trade. "There are but few fine buildings in the city and it appears to be a place of business rather than of pleasure," Bishop Henry Benjamin Whipple wrote. Another quipped that "there are no smart houses or equipages, nor indeed any demonstration of opulence" to be found in the town, "except huge ware-houses and a crowded harbor. Of amusements of any kind I heard nothing." One writer even found the business-centric atmosphere to be more like New York City's than other southern locale's, stating that "the business habits and manners of the people remind me of old Gotham." Few visitors to Mobile in this era failed to mention in some manner the centrality of the cotton trade to every facet of life.[18]

Of course, Mobile's antebellum economy had more to it than cotton, steamboats, and middlemen, but trade in other commodities paled in comparison in both volume and spectacle. Lumber products, such as logs, planks, staves, pitch, and turpentine, obtained from the region's vast interior forests and processed by local sawmills, ranked a distant second in terms of overall export value throughout the antebellum era. The port also sent tons of brick, leather, and lime to outside markets, among a range of products that together accounted for a rather small fraction of total export value. The Mobile riverfront also had a small shipbuilding industry, with varying levels of activity throughout this period. Overall, however, few locals were employed in manufacturing in the city or its surrounding region before 1860, and Mobile ranked as one of the least industrialized cities of its size in the South throughout the era. The city's economic health rose and fell with the one staple that became its lifeblood, weathering trying times of depression and boom times of regional financial growth in a roller-coaster ride of rise and decline that could make or break fortunes on a yearly basis.[19]

Rather than attempt diversification, the city doubled down on its role as a center of cotton exports by attempting to lure railroad lines to the port and counter the competition from locations that, previous to the invention of rail technology, played almost no part in the regional cotton trade. Railroad backers dreamed of increasing the value of the city's strategic location by connecting Mobile's port to the Ohio and Tennessee River valleys by railroad, potentially siphoning off some of the trade that otherwise went to New Orleans. The iron rails, they believed, could also expand the range of the cotton-producing southern interior, which might turn to Mobile as its primary outlet. Why this effort, begun in earnest in the years just before the Civil War, proved slow to materialize is a story for another day. But the bottom line is that by 1861, only one major rail line served the city. Throughout Mobile's antebellum era, the floating trade remained its economic lifeblood.[20]

Judging from the paucity of commentary in comparison to visitors' fascination with the cotton trade, the observers who left published records found the other components of Mobile's financial scene largely unremarkable. Few made an effort to comment on the city's hardware stores, bookshops, or retail clothing purveyors, save an occasional mention that they had passed a few such enterprises in the city's primary commercial district, centered on Dauphin Street. Restaurant patrons provided a smattering of mention; in the estimation of one, Mobile's eateries were "well supplied, and lunches at the saloons supply the inner man with game, Barataria Bay oysters, and all their accompaniments." A small number of writers found the city's market "abundantly supplied with provisions, fish, and game of every variety" and intriguing for its bustle and the variety of goods it offered. "There was nothing new to me but some fruit shops, in which were excellent oranges from Cuba, at six cents a piece, large pine apples . . . besides bananas and cocoa nuts in abundance," one traveler reported. "Fruit of every kind peculiar to the tropics is found here in greatest profusion," noted the writer and librarian Charles Lanman, who recalled seeing for sale "deer, wild turkeys, ducks and birds of the partridge tribe" alongside "saltwater trout, rockfish or striped bass, black bass, bream, sunfish, pike, redfish or red horse, sheepshead, salt-water mullet, buffalo or drum, flounder and flat fish, the common sucker, and catfish of every imaginable size." Overall, the authors make clear that Mobile's business infrastructure, concentrated to serve its primary commodity, defined the city's economic life and rendered it unique in the eyes of visitors. So captivating was the spectacle of the activity at one of the nation's busiest cotton ports that little else seemed worthy of notice.[21]

CHAPTER 5

Dangers

> It is fearful to witness the struggle between the love of gain, tempting the merchant to continue at his post, and the terror of the plague, which causes him to stand always prepared for sudden flight.
> —*Charles Lyell*

> One of the two great hotels here has just been burnt down, a thing that happens so regularly that it is considered a matter of course.
> —*John Oldmixon*

While Mobile's economy steadily grew in volume and regional importance throughout the antebellum period, it did so against a backdrop of threats that imperiled life, livelihoods, and reputation. Many came to regard the town, situated in a low-lying, warm, and humid area, as an unhealthy place to live because of the frequent epidemics of disease in the warmer months. One visitor deemed the city a vibrant place of trade situated in a "region of malaria."[1]

Few travelers ventured to Mobile in the summer if they could help it, for, as one visitor candidly observed, "the town is rather unhealthy the greater part of the summer, which drives away the greater part of the inhabitants." Numerous others commented on the pervasiveness of "intermittent fever, fever and ague, and other complaints" common to marshy areas such as Mobile's in the summer but less frequent in the winter. One of the few visitors who arrived during the heat of midsummer provided a disconcerting image that would have dissuaded others. He complained that upon debarking from his steamer "an atmosphere of horrible odors met us, permeating all the dirty streets. . . . The city was already quite empty, because whoever can leave in the summer flees before the threatening destruction." That the fall harvest of Mobile's primary export meant the bulk of its commercial activity took place in the winter months proved fortuitous for the city's development, to say the least.[2]

The dread disease known as yellow fever ranked as perhaps the most feared of the maladies that stalked early nineteenth-century Mobile. A severe viral infection marked by fever, chills, pain, and nausea, it earned its name from the associated liver damage that often caused the skin of victims to yellow. The illness brought quick and indiscriminate death, leaving those infected to suffer cruel agonies that often carried them to the grave in a matter of days after falling ill. It loomed as a particularly fearsome sickness because no cure existed and mystery surrounded its spread. In truth, it was most often communicated by the hordes of mosquitos that in summer invade humid lowland regions such as Mobile; people generally associated it with the swampy settings in which coastal communities were often located. They believed that decaying trash and waste in the streets or air passing over rotting vegetation in surrounding lowlands polluted the air in some way. They were on the right track, as those very things encouraged mosquitos and hence allowed for a faster spread of the disease, but the specifics eluded medical science at the time. Most writers, like the British visitor James Stuart, simply cautioned that Mobile's "neighboring swamps render it at certain seasons unhealthy."[3]

The state of medical knowledge was crude, and people often linked the causes and effects of illness in an almost superstitious manner. When the manager of the Mobile Theater died unexpectedly after an illness of just a few hours, having exhibited no previous symptoms, for example, some attributed the cause to "eating crabs for supper at a late hour." What most people came to understand through simple observation, however, was that the winter months were a relatively safe time to visit, but travelers regarded remaining in Mobile in the warmer months as foolhardy. "It is fearful to witness the struggle between the love of gain, tempting the merchant to continue at his post, and the terror of the plague, which causes him to stand always prepared for sudden flight," Charles Lyell, the Scottish genealogist, wrote. Like many, he understood that epidemics of communicable diseases were a veritable certainty to sweep the citizenry of Mobile periodically.[4]

Statistics bore him out in terrible fashion. Mobile experienced major outbreaks of yellow fever in 1819, 1825, 1837, 1839, 1843, 1853, and 1858—regular enough to threaten the health of city residents but not quite regular enough to make it a predictable occurrence. When the disease did strike, however, it could ravage the community with a vengeance. Whole families might die

The renowned Scottish geologist Charles Lyell was one of the world's most respected scientists when he visited Mobile in the 1840s. His books about his experiences in America, *Travels in North America* and *A Second Visit to the United States*, are filled with observations on American culture and society. Courtesy of the Library of Congress.

quietly in their houses in a period of days, and the city might lose as much as a third of its population to an epidemic few understood. In 1819 nearly three hundred Mobile residents died of yellow fever in just two months, and many more were sickened; in the fall of 1839 yellow fever took more than five hundred people and as much as 80 percent of the city's remaining population fled its limits at the height of the outbreak. In 1853 the city suffered a thousand cases of yellow fever. The disease killed so many during one episode in the 1840s that afterward several local Protestant denominations pooled their resources to organize an orphan asylum society to care for the numerous children left without parents. One visitor believed yellow fever and other contagious maladies were the defining characteristics of the city in its early years, claiming that during its colonial era and into its early American years the place seemed "little more than a focal spot for infection."[5]

Visitors' narratives recounted the horror stories they had heard about the disease as if they were tales of combat in some savage battle that had blighted

This symbolic depiction of the effects of yellow fever and its power to carry someone to the grave reveals the dread of the malady in cities such as Mobile. The sketch was created to show the ravages of the disease in Florida, and depicts "Columbia"—then the personification of the new nation—seemingly calling for help as a weakened victim sinks in despair. Trade, labeled on the box of merchandise at the bottom of the image, has been cast aside. Courtesy of the Library of Congress.

the town. "It is impossible for me to describe the dreadful mortality which took place," one visitor recorded the year after the terrible 1819 outbreak. "While walking the streets my amazement has been, not why so many died, but how so many, in such low and filthy situations, could have survived." Another writer who visited later, and perhaps was informed by stories of locals who had survived a devastating epidemic, noted the brutal efficiency with which yellow fever dispatched those who contracted it. Cautioning that more than 10 percent of those exposed to the illness died during a typical outbreak, he wrote of its effects in simple but chilling words: "It is a very rapid fever, cutting off the sufferer in four days." Some travelers, who in general avoided Mobile during the dangerous months of late summer, expressed a degree of disbelief that a substantial portion of its population would choose to remain there all year. "Great is the anxiety of those who then remain in the city," wrote one visitor, capturing a truth but apparently oblivious that most Mobilians did not have the wherewithal to keep two residences. After a sojourn there in 1860, one guest summarized the situation bluntly: "The yellow fever epidemic is a very serious drawback to the idea of a residence in Mobile."[6]

Yellow fever was not the only malady that struck Mobilians in the antebellum era. At least one traveler, who arrived just as the city was struggling to recover from an epidemic of cholera, an intestinal virus caused by drinking contaminated water or poor sanitation, was disconcerted to note that handbills with recipes for cures and advertisements for coffins "meet one at every turn." Others, astonished at the city's level of progress, given its challenging health environment, cautioned that it might never develop much further as a residential area. "Mobile appears to be stationary," observed the businessman and politician Robert Russell in his book about North America's agriculture and climate. He reached this conclusion because of the panoply of diseases that "rages with great virulence in summer."[7]

Instead of abandoning the city, Mobile's residents fought back. They did everything from draining swamps and eliminating stagnant water whose noxious air many believed to be the origin of some maladies to eating certain foods and drinking certain alcoholic spirits that some believed might help ward off illness. They attempted to keep streets swept free of decaying piles of trash, "attention to cleanliness having been rendered indispensable from the fatality with which the yellow fever used to visit Mobile," noted one observer who was in the city between outbreaks. Some even took the advice of doctors who advised taking a bath as often as weekly during the warm season to ward off illness. Mobile had vaccination programs and built "pest houses" for those suffering from maladies such as smallpox who could be quarantined; eventually, the city built a hospital. Perhaps the best illustration of the spirit of resolve and concern for other citizens was that, as early as the 1830s, business leaders and civic groups volunteered to work with and support organizations such as the Samaritan Society and the Can't Get Away Club that provided medical aid and essential services during an epidemic when large portions of the population fled the city.[8]

A few Mobilians simply moved to higher ground a short distance west of the city around Spring Hill, where, they believed, the small change in elevation afforded a healthier environment but allowed them to be close enough to the city that they still could participate in its commercial operations and social opportunities. Originally viewed as a "healthy and not unpleasant summer retreat," the wooded hills west of town, which had several springs of cool water, quickly became one of Mobile's most unusual suburbs in the first decades of the nineteenth century. As early as 1822, a few hundred people were already living in the Spring Hill area, and by the 1830s one visitor found along the "healthy plains" to the west of Mobile's commercial core a growing community "to which they retire both to avoid the extreme heat of the summer and the yellow fever." Through it all, city promoters, and not a few objective visitors, believed that even with the periodic outbreaks of disease (which also struck many other communities), the "situation of the town is, on the whole, very favourable to health." Few would have contested the general opinion of the day that Mobile ranked as much healthier than New Orleans, for example. Yet the Crescent City's reputation for unhealthiness did little to stymie its robust growth during the antebellum era, and in the end Mobile's reputation seemed to affect its trajectory only marginally. Like New Orleans, Mobile's strategic location virtually demanded it be a place of trade at the time, inconvenient outbreaks of disease notwithstanding.[9]

Of the multiple other threats to health and livelihood that stalked Mobile in the early nineteenth century, few ranked as feared or as destructive as fire. Like most cities of the era, antebellum Mobile featured an assortment of closely built wooden structures, many of which shared walls along their continuous street frontage. Given the lack of piped water and the ubiquity of open fires for cooking, heating, and light, a small accidental conflagration could spread with lightning speed and destroy large swaths of the city before anything could be done to slow its progress. Such calamities, of varying destructiveness, struck Mobile on several occasions before the Civil War. Few were more memorable or destructive than those of 1820, 1827, and 1839. "On Friday evening [August 11, 1820] about 1 o'clock, the inhabitants of this city were alarmed by the cry of fire, which was found to have originated in the cotton press and warehouse belonging to Col. L. Judson," a newspaper reported. "In a few minutes, in spite of every exertion," the fire "communicated to the adjacent buildings ... [and] from these buildings the flames spread with great rapidity to buildings on each side of Dauphin Street, the whole of which, from Water Street to Royal Street, were in a few hours reduced to ashes." The same report noted that the flames spread with such speed that even "property removed from the stores was burned in the street," that is, it caught fire even there.[10]

The 1827 fire scorched several blocks in the heart of the city, from the riverfront to St. Emmanuel Street, and devastated the area from St. Francis Street to Government Street. More than two-thirds of the city's central business district burned in the blaze, which by most estimates consumed more than 150 commercial buildings and homes. The 1839 conflagration laid waste to an even larger swath of the city, charring dozens of blocks west of Water Street, including both sides of Dauphin Street, and north to Franklin Street. More than a third of the city's structures went up in flames or were destroyed in the attempt to arrest the inferno's progress by depriving it of additional fuel. An unknown number died in the disaster that, according to one visitor who saw the aftermath, simply "laid the greater part of [Mobile] in ashes."[11]

Destruction by Fire of Pennsylvania Hall,
On the night of the 17th May, 1838

This print depicts a conflagration in Philadelphia in the 1830s, but it shows the type of disastrous fire that swept through close-packed, predominantly wooden urban centers such as Mobile at the time. Courtesy of the Library of Congress.

In the aftermath of such terrible infernos, the city instituted building regulations meant to minimize their recurrence. The city mandated brick construction in the city center to replace the traditional wood-frame buildings that went up like kindling in sweeping blazes. By 1840 municipal officials had actually banned all-wood construction in the core of the city, and they had taken steps to begin widening and straightening Mobile's downtown streets. As a result Mobile appeared as a new city, markedly different after each blaze, both because of what had been lost and the nature of what had replaced it. Of course, even brick buildings have wooden interior elements, and fire remained a serious threat to the city, especially given the poor water pressure and inadequate equipment available to fire companies. It is fair to say that Mobile underwent several dramatic alterations of its physical appearance between 1820 and 1845, with each makeover rendering it more resistant to fire by degrees. As rich as the city's architectural legacy is today, fire consumed hundreds of early nineteenth-century structures in the early antebellum period. With more regulation of building materials and increased fire response services as the years progressed—as early as 1819 volunteer fire companies had formed in Mobile, and six formed in the 1830s alone—fire became a less-feared specter haunting the city's development, at least in terms of its ability to erase entire sections of town in a single outbreak.[12]

Visitors, especially those arriving in the 1820s and 1830s, could not help but comment on the ghastly effects and the startling regularity of large fires in Mobile. Basil Hall, the Scottish scientist who arrived only a short time after the ruinous 1827 fire, noted that "on the 7th of April, we reached what *remained* of Mobile, for the town had been almost entirely burnt down not quite six months before." James Silk Buckingham, the Englishman who stopped in the city during his 1839 tour of the southern United States, recorded that during his stay of a few days at least two fires of a serious nature broke out. One burned a single warehouse on Royal Street, while another damaged several buildings on Government Street. Another visitor, taken aback by the traces of widespread destruction still evident years after one of the larger fires to sweep through Mobile, observed with incredulity how the city seemed to be growing steadily "notwithstanding a great fire which some time ago destroyed a very considerable part of the town." Others, such as the Scottish writer Thomas Hamilton, who evidently heard gory details of

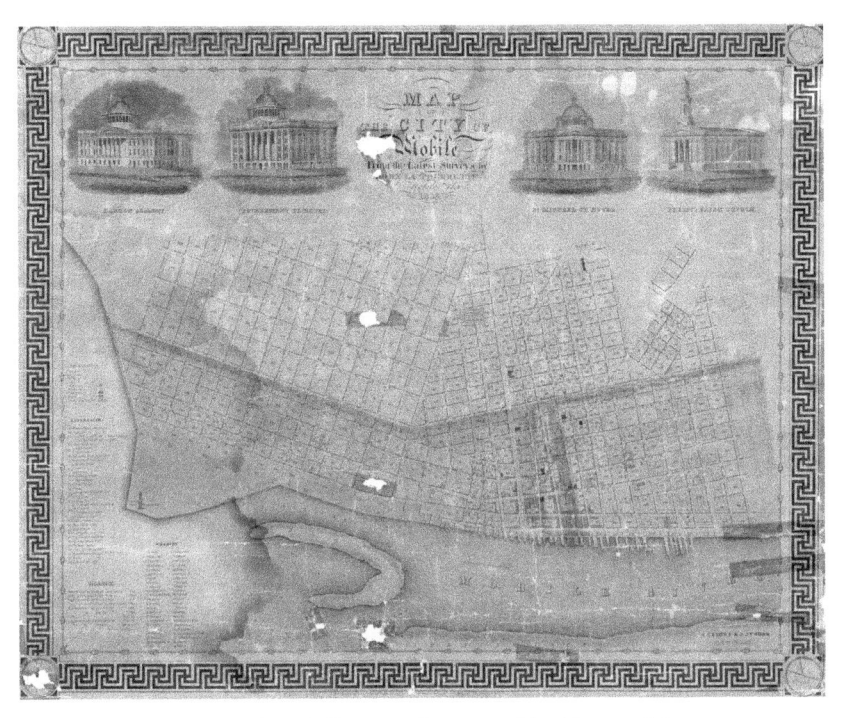

Map of Mobile in 1838, by John La Tourette. Courtesy of the Library of Congress

the devastating effects of major recent blazes during his time in the city, was surprised that, just a few years after a large fire, he could find "but few traces of the conflagration."[13]

Travelers were of course keenly aware of the loss of the city's hotels in the larger blazes that destroyed entire blocks of the community, leading to inconvenience at best and sometimes abbreviated stays. "One of the two great hotels here has just been burnt down," remarked one frustrated tourist on arrival in Mobile in the late 1840s. He noted with resignation that the occurrence had become "a thing that happens so regularly that it is considered a matter of course" in the city. Yet visitors arriving in time to see the effects of new building regulations and the practical rebirth of the city in the wake of the fires marveled at what amounted to a new community. "The conflagrations, with which [Mobile] has been visited of late years, have contributed to its embellishment. Instead of the former log-huts, rows of fine brick houses are now to be seen ... [and] well-planned thoroughfares, made of oyster and other shells."[14]

Other dangers that lurked in antebellum times had much more to do with machismo than microbes or conflagrations but were part of the city's milieu and on occasion proved just as deadly. Visitor accounts are studded with mentions of public drunkenness, fistfights, gunfights, stabbings, and even reports of "robbers, scoundrels, and incendiaries" who were operating in the city. Some were events the travelers heard about in conversation with locals and described as recent but in actuality had occurred many months or more previously. That they mentioned them in the course of describing a city they visited for only a few days might leave the impression Mobile harbored more dangers than it perhaps did. Still, a few travelers did come uncomfortably close to violence during their time in Mobile and could verify that the city had its fair share of disorder and lawlessness.[15]

The actor Tyrone Power, for example, recounted hearing a scuffle in the audience while on stage during the performance of a play in Mobile. Only afterward did he learn a man had been stabbed and died during the production. The performance had been allowed to continue despite what the audience apparently viewed as a momentary disorder. Power may have been surprised to hear of how matter-of-factly the event had been dealt with, but he certainly would not have been startled to hear that a murder had occurred in a city he had visited on multiple occasions and that had seen rather well-publicized episodes of violence. Newspapers in New Orleans, among others in the region and perhaps beyond, carried stories about some of the more outrageous events in Alabama's largest city that would have come to the attention of visitors. For example, two days of unrest following a mayoral election featured alcohol-fueled belligerents and resulted in multiple fights and at least two murders; this news would certainly have made the rounds at regional steamboat landings and stagecoach stops. But even during the same stint in town when the audience member was murdered, Tyrone Power wrote nonchalantly of hearing that a gunfight involving the alleged theft of enslaved people had broken out between plantation owners. He did not record whether he heard of any deaths resulting from the affair. The *New Orleans Daily Picayune* reported the murder of a man by another after some sort of altercation at a dinner both had attended—only one of two murders the reporter heard had occurred during his short stay. It is easy to see why,

Tyrone Power was one of the most famous actors to visit Mobile. He recorded his experiences in the city in *Impressions of America*. Courtesy of the Library of Congress.

one traveler ventured, few weeks seemed to pass in Mobile without "outrages which are shocking to persons of correct feeling."[16]

Blaming the effects of strong drink on agitated minds for many of the episodes of violence in antebellum Mobile would have been easy, and certainly the assumption many made about the root cause of mayhem in the city contains some truth. The city was home to several establishments that catered especially to dock workers and transient sailors looking to blow off steam. And at the time men who were openly carrying large knives and guns on city streets were not uncommon. Yet it is not clear that the city had any more violence per capita than other cities its size. Mobile, in fact, may have had less because its police force became professionalized before the Civil War and by most accounts appears to have reined in the worst of the excesses during the city's rowdy early American period. Between the 1820s and 1830s Mobile's police force morphed from an ad hoc city guard to an official municipal organization. By the 1850s the force appears to have cut the frequency and extent of the drunken frolics and brawls so common to the streets of port cities late at night. Still, some visitors believed the police kept order selectively by area of the city and simply looked the other way in the parts of town where late-night entertainment could be found. One visitor claimed to have seen entire districts of the city featuring "dance-houses of the lowest order, where lawlessness, indecency, and debauchery reigned supreme" with little or no intervention by law enforcement. The same observer, perhaps exaggerating to make his point, wrote of also witnessing several drunken brawls on city streets, noting that city police seemingly were "compelled to stand calmly by until the combatants had pummeled one another to their heart's satisfaction." Like any large community of the time, Mobile had its share of unruliness and violence, episodes that were discussed widely and could leave a bad impression if they occurred during a visitor's stay.[17]

Such depictions, however exaggerated, contributed to a general idea that Mobile could be, at least on occasion, a potentially dangerous place for unwary visitors who might find themselves in the wrong place at the wrong time. Some could be forgiven if they were surprised at just how well Mobile managed to increase its population and economic activity, given the incidence of violence, disease, and fire. "It is a matter of astonishment," Buckingham wrote, "that with such elements of demoralization and destruction so constantly and actively at work, a city could ever make progress." Yet it did and in doing so fostered the development of a lively social scene that would become an intriguing focal point for visitors.[18]

CHAPTER 6

People and Lifestyles

> You can see as great varieties of character in the streets of Mobile as in any city of its size in the union.
> —*Henry B. Whipple*

> It is an extravagant, joyous and free and easy town.... Sporting characters, thoroughbred and fast horses, and lovely women are as familiar as household words. Warm-hearted, it seems to me, are all its citizens.
> —*Charles Lanman*

A casual glance at society in antebellum Mobile through the eyes of its visitors can leave the impression that it was a stereotypical southern town of yesteryear, straight out of the hagiographic accounts of an Old South we now know never existed. "It is an extravagant, joyous and free and easy town," wrote the librarian Charles Lanman during his stay in the 1850s, for example. Such estimations were based on actual observation, no doubt, but the city had much more to it than the trappings of wealth that a small portion of its population exhibited. Visitor accounts were not meant as piercing sociological analysis, but they nonetheless reveal that Mobile was a diverse and colorful place with a population that at any given point featured the largest population of foreign-born residents in the state and more relative newcomers than deep-rooted families. Visitors' observations certainly did not include all aspects of Mobile society, but collectively they portray daily life in the city in a revealing way.[1]

Rapid population growth characterized Mobile before the Civil War. When the city first came under American control in 1813, it had only about 500 people, but within a decade its population had more than doubled to 1,200. According to some estimates, during the busy winter trading seasons of the early 1820s, the city may have hosted more than 2,500 people. The city had doubled its residential population by the end of the 1820s, and by the late 1830s, when a visitor wrote that "the rush of strangers into this city continues about as large as ever," it had quadrupled. After a relative lull in expansion in the trying economic times of the 1840s, Mobile welcomed the 1850s with a resident population of more than 20,000. An 1855 census revealed the city was home to more than 20,000 white citizens, approximately 8,000 enslaved people, and more than 1,000 free Blacks. When the Civil War began in 1861, Mobile had nearly 30,000 permanent residents and ranked as the fourth-largest city in the Confederacy.[2]

A few special aspects characterized Mobile's population and drew comments from the city's visitors—it fluctuated seasonally, was comprised in large part of newcomers, and was more diverse than most communities in the larger region. Numerous travelers noted that the number of Mobile inhabitants rose in the winter and fell in the summer. Mobile's population could as much as double between November and May, the peak time for selling and shipping cotton and the healthiest time of year. Many of the most influential business leaders lived in town for less than half the year, leaving in early summer for extended vacations or stays in second homes elsewhere to avoid the sultry temperatures, high humidity, slow economic times, and mosquito-borne disease. Numerous other people involved in the city's cotton trade descended on the town only during the trading season; at about the time of the first frost, many left their plantations in the interior for extended stays in Mobile with their families.[3]

The languid community of the summer seemed to spring to frenzied life when the temperature began to moderate. Downtown shops and offices pulsed with activity as the harbor filled with the ships of the cotton trade and workers swarmed the wharves as they loaded and unloaded the staple and prepared it for overseas shipment. Otherwise empty hotels were suddenly packed, previously shuttered restaurants filled with the sounds of conversation and the clanking of silverware and dishes, and theaters opened for a season of performances that drew crowds numbering in the hundreds every evening. Erstwhile quiet, dusty streets became thronged with horse-drawn carriages, and nearly deserted sidewalks became human cordons of focused businessmen and leisure shoppers during the day or people looking for an evening's entertainment at night. The city's numerous grog shops and houses of entertainment, where those in search of such could find strong drink, play games of chance, and, should they desire, buy a night's female companionship, also swung open their doors.[4]

The Mobile City Market in 1857. Courtesy of the Historic Mobile Preservation Society.

The radical transformation from lethargy to vitality left many tourists with the impression that Mobile was a distinctly seasonal community. "During the summer months the business nearly ceases," one observer noted, as "all who can, leave the city." They regarded the city as "remarkable for possessing a shifting population." The "winter transient population" of merchants and laborers was one of the city's hallmarks. John Morris, who stayed through spring in Mobile one year, recorded the dramatic change as summer arrived: "The hot weather had struck upon us, mercantile establishments were closed; steamers were laying up, commerce, which had thrilled the city in every artery with busy life, was in its last throes. Familiar faces that had lately thronged our streets and public places had disappeared; 'fly time' had arrived." This reality sometimes led to exaggeration by describing its extremes. In the estimation of one visitor in the early 1840s, "Mobile is a town of about 15,000 inhabitants in the winter & 2,500 in summer." These and other such approximations perhaps embellished (but only slightly) the reality of dramatic differences in seasonal populations that made Mobile an unusual city in which to live, do business, or visit during the antebellum era.[5]

Because Mobile's population—at least during the business season—grew so rapidly in just a few decades, the city seemed always to be filled with newcomers. Residents who had lived in the city for a decade were considered longtimers. The city's population also was young. Life expectancies in this period were much shorter than those of today, but for the most part it was the young, ambitious—and often single—who journeyed to new communities on the make in search of economic opportunity. In Mobile's early years, especially, bachelors comprised a large portion of its population. This began to change as families steadily became a greater part of community life, but in 1840 the city still had twice as many residents aged twenty to thirty as any other age group. In the city's early years, family history counted for little. Few indeed were those residents who had inherited family wealth or influence, because so few had been in town long enough to accumulate either. The former Mobile mayor Addin Lewis had arrived from Connecticut shortly after the United States annexed the city. When he retired from public life in 1829 at age forty-nine, he was among the oldest and longest-tenured community leaders.[6]

Antebellum Mobile featured, by the state's standards at the time, a diverse population in terms of ethnic background. In 1860 nearly a third of the city's residents had been born in another country and accounted for more than 60 percent of all foreign-born residents in Alabama at the time. These first-generation Americans served as a prominent part of the city's free male labor force, comprising as much as half of all these workers. People whose roots were in Ireland, Scotland, France, and Germany were present in numbers that allowed each group to form its own distinct communities. The city's Irish population was especially large, making up nearly half of the city's foreign-born population; it supported a robust Hibernian Society that, among a variety of undertakings, staged a vigorous celebration of St. Patrick's Day each year. At one point in the antebellum era, the Battle House Hotel employed more than seventy Irish workers—a majority of its workforce. Those of distinct European backgrounds formed several other social organizations in antebellum Mobile. The city's German residents, while not as numerous as the Irish, formed a militia unit and a local Turner's Society (a German American organization that promoted German culture and physical fitness) and staged May Day activities.[7]

As a result of its exceptional ethnic diversity, Mobile retained what many visitors referred to as a "foreign cast" throughout the antebellum period. Some even remarked that the city seemed in some ways more like an old European town than a typical American community of the period. The naturalist Philip Henry Gosse spoke for many when he expressed how, during his short visit to Mobile in the late 1830s, he was "struck by an unusual character, a certain something of a foreign appearance which was forcibly evident... in the streets a little removed from the more commercial part of the city." Even at the time, many observers understood the city's population diversity as a testament to its distinctive history and heritage. Literate visitors were well aware in the mid-1810s that what had been a small colonial outpost featuring residents of French, British, Spanish, and African heritage, and numerous combinations of all these, became a magnet for a new wave of immigrants from Europe and elsewhere in America. Alexander Mackay, like several other visitors, saw the city's history written in the unusual assemblage of its people. "In the character of a portion of the population, as well as in other circumstances, the stranger can see proofs of the comparatively recent annexation of this portion of the country to the Republican confederacy," he wrote. While guests may have conflated Mobile's colonial heritage and mid-eighteenth-century ethnic makeup a bit more than the facts merited, they were nonetheless aware that the city was home to many newcomers from Europe who, in the estimation of one visitor, "came here to make money."[8]

Visitors' accounts of pre–Civil War Mobile describe the city's foreign-born population as a prominent part of their experience in town. John S. C. Abbott, for example, remembered how "Irish and the Germans seem to do nearly all the work of the streets" of the city, while Charles Lanman noted that many of the butchers and peddlers whose shops he visited were of "French or Spanish extractions." Joseph Holt Ingraham complained about the dispositions of many Irish servants he found in town: "I can never understand them, nor they me, and this irritates their natural quickness, and they sometimes become exceedingly disagreeable." Others noted the several Scottish bakers in the city, including one who, the Scottish writer Thomas Hamilton learned, had made his way to Mobile after arriving in New York in pursuit of opportunity. The man expressed his satisfaction that in America he "need have no fears about his family, for he has plenty to give them in the mean time; and if they live, they will soon be able to provide for themselves," Hamilton reported. The man's only complaint was that in the United States he had been "obliged to mingle with a most profane and godless set. He lamented that [he] could not hear the gospel preached, as he has been accustomed to, and the profanation of the Sabbath is most awful." Frederick Law Olmsted believed that the numerous British merchants present in the city during his visit "affect[ed] the character of the society, considerably," lending their customs, manners, and deportment to its culture. Yet few could describe antebellum Mobile as anything but an American community. To be sure, the many residents born in Europe may have accounted for a greater percentage of the population than in other cities, but Mobile still was representative of a nation full of immigrants. "It bears but few traces either of its French or its Spanish founders," Charles Mackay noted. Even though "some of its most enterprising citizens are English and Scotch, attracted to it by its business connections with Liverpool and Glasgow," visitors like Mackay still described Mobile as American in culture and appearance.[9]

Mobile's racial diversity was even more distinctive than the ethnicity of its European-born community, and the binary nature of the city's society did not escape attention. (Chapter 7 discusses visitors' reaction to the institution of slavery.) The assemblage of races and nationalities, however, struck tourists as one of the identifying features of Mobile. Charles Lanman straightforwardly summed up the city's racial heterogeneity by describing it as "negroes of every age and shade of color and an occasional group of Choctaw Indians" mixed in with Americans and Europeans. With all these people of different backgrounds present, he pronounced Mobile to "have a sufficient variety."[10]

Guests in Mobile were inspired to record their impressions of the large Choctaw camp that periodically sprang to life just outside the city after the mid-1830s. A landmark tourist attraction for sightseers, the camp served as the gathering place for a community of Native Americans who had escaped removal but lingered near the city for the economic opportunities it afforded them. The encampment appears to have been a seasonal affair, populated during the winter months only, a base from which the men of the tribe could hunt deer and turkey to sell in Mobile's market and the women could sell lightwood and knickknacks in the city. The camp represented the tattered remnant of a proud people reduced to becoming a tourist attraction for part of the year just to survive in a region where many assumed they no longer lived. The camp formed a poignant spectacle of poor people still fiercely independent and clinging to traditional ways even if often "half fed and half clothed," a *New York Times* reporter wrote. The reporter pointed out the significance of the Choctaws' presence in a rapidly growing area of American settlement. And he attempted to place the camp in context by movingly describing it as a holdout of a people "fast passing from the earth."[11]

The camp appeared to be a genuine but temporary Native American village, and it transfixed visitors, most of whom had never seen anything like it. They found it to be both simple and exotic, and several visited it multiple times during their short stays in Mobile. The British artist Victoria Welby, who perhaps wrote the most about the camp, described it as a few dozen "bark huts" arranged in a field west of town. Women within the encampment were engaged in a variety of domestic chores such as "pounding Indian corn for their hominy" and minding an assemblage of kettles and cooking pots "smoking about in the sun, slung to three sticks as a tripod." Children ran about the area, some playing and some helping their mothers with small tasks, and men returned from and resumed short excursions into the nearby forest to pursue the game that would provide meat for their own consumption and to sell at Mobile's market.[12]

All, especially the hunters, would quietly inspect their visitors as the Choctaw went about their daily routines. Some offered to sell jewelry and handicrafts they had produced. Victoria Welby reported seeing her host, the local resident Octavia LeVert, buy a necklace from a Choctaw girl that was "composed of shells, teeth, bones, tufts of hair, bits of horn, wire, glass, beads, &c." The Choctaws' silver headbands, turbans, beaded moccasins, and clothing adorned with bird feathers fascinated Welby and other visitors. Only a few visitors left descriptions of the interiors of Choctaw lodges; whether only a few had the opportunity to see their living quarters or only a few chose to record their impressions is not clear. Welby believed the interiors of the Choctaw huts were "in a state of confusion beyond all description, filled with babies, dogs, pieces of cotton, baskets, Indian corn, hunting horns, wampumbelts, blankets, pots, pans, dried meat, guns, bows and arrows, deer-skins, raccoon-skins." In one she was amused to find, of all things, a broken accordion. Visitors found the Choctaw to be "a singular people," with everything about their encampment speaking of a proud but poor community adrift in a world from which they had been tragically displaced. The Choctaws' provisional camp revealed them to be neither fully accepting of American ways nor completely able to live their lives traditionally, and everything about the place seemed temporary, ad hoc, and speaking to an uncertain future.[13]

Visitors nonetheless discerned a certain dignity about the Choctaw and were captivated by their exoticness and independence. Lady Emmeline Stuart Wortley described them as having "a certain nobleness of look," noting "the women are ... very handsome." The "very handsome features" of the men likewise struck Victoria Welby as the embodiment of what people like her, who had only read about American Indians, had imagined. "He was completely the North American Indian," she gushed about a hunter she encountered. "A beautifully chiseled aquiline nose, immense and sleepy-looking eyes, and a most classic mouth. . . . The grandeur and sternness of the expression which pervaded his whole countenance were extremely striking." During a visit to the camp, Welby convinced a Choctaw woman to sit for a portrait and was moved by her: "Her eyes, which were the deepest black, shone with a most brilliant lustre through her long eyelashes; and her mouth more resembled an opening rose-bud than anything else I can think of."[14]

Some travelers perceived a sort of fierce independence in the Choctaw and remarked on their composure and self-confidence in a setting in which most visitors judged the Native Americans to be supremely out of place. Thomas Hamilton remarked on the general poverty of the Choctaw in and around Mobile, for example, but admired how they nonetheless appeared "patient under suffering." He believed "something of their original grace and spirit seemed to cling to them" but acknowledged he had learned little directly from them about their situation, although he tried. "I often attempted to converse with them," he remembered, "but their taciturnity was not to be overcome." John Oldmixon would have seconded Hamilton's assessment. In his words, "they speak to nobody, rarely smile, or seem to take the smallest interest in anything going on about them."[15]

Choctaws became a common sight on Mobile's streets. During his stay in town in the 1850s, Charles Lanman estimated "the number of Indians who spend much of their time in Mobile, but who live in the neighboring pine woods" numbered "about a thousand." The Choctaw men who did "a little hunting for the market," he surmised, made it "their principal business to deck themselves in bright colors and hang about the market or hotels." Lanman observed a few men and boys collecting a dime or two from people astounded by the Choctaws' remarkable skill with the bow and arrow, shooting "at a mark" of exceptional difficulty and rarely missing. One observer claimed to have seen a Choctaw boy hit a coin with an arrow at a distance of sixty yards during one of these demonstrations. During his visit to Mobile in the 1840s, the accomplished French composer and pianist Henri Herz wrote of the novelty of having part of his audience comprised of Choctaw Indians. He wrote of being flattered when told that after hearing him play they considered him "a spirit descended from the world of harmony to instruct mankind."[16]

Lanman praised the women as "industrious, and [they] manage to keep themselves quite comfortable by selling bundles of fat pine for lighting fires, and beautiful willow baskets." These bundles of fire starters, which the Choctaw called *chumpa*, became a common article on the streets of the city during the winter. "The women, young and old," Charles Mackay wrote, "are often to be seen in Mobile with bundles of fire-wood on their backs, which they sell in the streets, crying with a melancholy intonation 'chumpa! chumpa!'" Even visitors who devoted scarcely a sentence of their published narratives to the Choctaw presence in Mobile noted the pervasiveness of chumpa sellers in the city and even in the corridors of its hotels. They "went about the streets selling wood, which they carried in small billets, bound on their backs," noted one, while another remembered Choctaw girls had knocked at the door of her hotel room to offer the bundles.[17]

Visitors made anthropological observations about other people they encountered in Mobile. One noted,

> You can see as great varieties of character in the streets of Mobile as in any city of its size in the union. Clerks of all shapes and sizes; white & red haired men, staid thinking men, and brainless fops. Here goes a staid, demure faced priest and behind him is a dashy gambler. Here goes a quiet Quaker merchant and there is your Mississippi 'buster.' . . . Here is a sailor just on shore with a pocket full of rocks ready for devilment of any kind and there is a beggar in rags. Pretty Creoles, pale faced sewing girls, painted vice, big headed and little headed men, tall anatomies and short Falstaffs, are all seen.

Unable to characterize the population within a single narrow category, the British businessman and writer Adam Hodgson termed the city's heterogeneous inhabitants as "of a most miscellaneous kind," linked together only by their "profaneness, licentiousness, and ferocity." Others were perplexed by the assortment of individuals they came across who were, Frederick Law Olmsted observed, "more than any people I had ever seen . . . unrateable by dress, taste, forms, and expenditures." He expressed his surprise at finding, "united in the same individual, the self-possession and confidence of the well-equipped gentleman, and the coarseness and low tastes of the uncivilized boor." Another, only half in jest, recounted that he found four "descriptions of animated nature" in Mobile—"cotton shippers, doctors, alligators, and undertakers."[18]

As to social life in Mobile, visitors found both much to admire and a good deal to scorn. As might be expected in a prosperous commercial city, tourists observed ostentatious displays of wealth among a certain portion of the population and stood impressed by the social trappings of that money. Guests commented that Mobile was home to a significant number of individuals "to the manor born . . . genuine Southerners by birth and feeling" who were enjoying the privileges of wealth. Large houses with well-kept grounds, lavish parties with impeccably dressed attendees, and extravagant hospitality were all in evidence among what some described as a local aristocracy of well-to-do merchant families. Ingraham professed to be "delighted with the society of Mobile" and "the refined hospitality and cordial attention" on display. In perhaps a bit of hyperbole, he gushed that he "found the Mobileans among the most elegant people we have ever associated with." Another visitor reported, "The higher orders partake in much of the hospitality and elegance of Charleston and Savannah," adding that, "in this rank of society great intelligence, morality, and honour are to be found." Others echoed these sentiments, describing Mobile society as "frank and agreeable," the city as the home of "beautiful women" and men possessing "intelligence and frank manner." Oldmixon noted, "From the little I have seen of it, I should say that Mobile possesses a great share of beauty and accomplishments in its women, and pleasing manners among the leading men."[19]

But the collective description of antebellum society in Mobile from the pages of visitor narratives is not one characterized by general wealth and refinement alone. Rather, observers found what they believed to be excessive displays of boorish and unprincipled behavior by a population composed for the most part of "the most dissolute and unprincipled of men." The Scottish-born Canadian journalist Alexander Mackay wrote, "It would be difficult to find anywhere a more hospitable set of people than the better portion of the population of Mobile, although a large proportion of the lower orders are prone to a dissoluteness of manners equal to that characteristic of the corresponding classes of the more immoral of European capitals." One visitor who claimed to have been in Mobile several times likened the city to nearby New Orleans, describing both as "hot-beds of sensuality" in an indictment of Gulf Coast social life. He claimed the customs, habits, and vice he witnessed in Mobile "debase the mind, enervate the body, and weaken the ligaments which bind well regulated and virtuous societies together, thereby causing a premature death to virtue, public tranquility and domestic happiness." While acknowledging "there are many here who prefer literature and its rational enjoyments to the theatre and gay revels," Bishop Henry Whipple summed up "the tone of society in Mobile" as "very gay and to a certain extent dissipated." Yet another claimed to have seen more of "men than of manners" during his brief stay in town. A visitor who provided an explanatory synopsis of the dichotomy of Mobile society believed there were two distinct classes of southerners, both much in evidence in the port city and "as different from each other as light is from darkness." One could be described as genteel and graceful, the other crude and unpolished. Few seemed to find a group between these extremes.[20]

Visitors' accounts of their experiences in the dining rooms of Mobile's hotels, restaurants, and private homes perhaps best reveal their perception of a duality in city society. Some travelers described being invited into the leisurely world of the city's wealthy and its nicer establishments, where dinner tables groaned with delicious local seafood and smooth French wine. Lunch seems to have been the largest meal of the day, often served in the early afternoon. Many other guests in the city, experiencing only the crowded public accommodations available to most travelers, painted a different picture of repasts in Mobile. Some found the speed with which meals were dispatched in public gatherings baffling and a point of interest—Hodgson, the British businessman, averred that five or six minutes was the normal time spent enjoying a meal in the city. Others declared that the warnings they had been given elsewhere—that the farther south one proceeded "the tables and beds would get worse and worse, and the charges be higher and higher"—were true enough. One frustrated traveler noted that, in his estimation, service at Mobile's dining establishments was abysmal, a place where rudeness at the table was all too common and servers frequently ignored requests. Perhaps

A native of New York and an Episcopal priest, Henry Benjamin Whipple served for more than forty years as the bishop of Minnesota. His account of his travels in the South was published as *Bishop Whipple's Southern Diary* in the 1960s. Courtesy of the Library of Congress.

his was a singular experience, but more than one complained of "the same overloaded table, bad cookery, and worse attendance" as characterizing their dining experiences in the city.[21]

Uncouth behavior aside, before the Civil War Mobile hosted a variety of civic groups, social clubs, and charitable organizations that played a key part in its society and gave evidence of the city's urban sophistication. Though few travelers said much about them, as early as the 1820s, the city could claim among its philanthropic organizations those providing support for the needs of various portions of its population such as the Female Benevolent Society, the Auxiliary Tract Society, and the Hibernian Benevolent Society. Later in the period, the Ladies Bethel Society, which dedicated itself to seeing to the needs of sailors visiting the city's busy port, supported the establishment of a library, boardinghouse, and a community worship center, known as a Bethel, that hosted religious services for multiple denominations. The Baymen's Society offered assistance to stevedores working in Mobile's harbor facilities. Serving the needs of those with intellectual interests were literary groups, such as the Franklin Society, which served as a sort of forum for academic inquiry in the arts and sciences. By the later decades of the prewar period, Mobile had begun to fully embrace the Mardi Gras tradition and the mystic societies that staged carnival celebrations came to play a progressively more important role in the city's social life. Membership in fire and militia companies, while providing important services for the community, also offered the men of Mobile opportunities for social networking.[22]

The city's many churches constituted another influential set of social organizations in antebellum Mobile, and their diversity reflected the city's growing population. Throughout most of the town's colonial history and well into the American period, a Catholic church stood as the lone physical structure in the city that had been built for worship. The French and Spanish had recognized Catholicism as the official state religion during their occupations, and the British, though officially promoting the Anglican Church, never got around to building a worship facility. During the visit of Adam Hodgson in the early 1820s, for example, Mobile, "to the disgrace of Protestant America," contained no proper "Protestant place of worship." By the end of 1823, however, one had at last appeared in the city. Known as the Union Church, the Gothic Revival structure was used by multiple congregations until each

Christ Church as it appeared in 1840. Courtesy of the Historic Mobile Preservation Society.

could build its own. At the end of the antebellum period, Mobile could claim more than two dozen houses of worship, including those serving Episcopal, Methodist, Presbyterian, Baptist, and Unitarian congregations in addition to a magnificent Catholic cathedral. A few offered separate campuses for Black members, and some policed segregated seating by race. A Jewish synagogue added to the diversity of the city's ecclesiastical architecture. In 1846 a Jewish congregation in Mobile, Sha'arai Shomayim, held a dedication for the Emanual Street Synagogue, Alabama's first. Mobile had had a small but prominent

Jewish community since the 1820s, including a noted early doctor (Solomon Mordecai), a city councilman and acting mayor (Israel Jones), and several prominent businessmen and professionals. The congregation was founded in 1844 and worshipped in private homes before building the temple.[23]

Government Street Presbyterian Church in the 1830s, as depicted in the margins of Tourette's map of Mobile. Courtesy of the Library of Congress.

Mobile's churches became important parts of the city's infrastructure as the antebellum period progressed. Few bothered to make much comment on the city's houses of worship in the first decades of the era, likely because they were so few and a rather unremarkable assemblage in architectural terms. One early visitor to Mobile, for example, was less than complimentary when describing the Catholic church he encountered in the mid-1820s, then still the largest such structure in the city. He described it as resembling a barn, noting that within "it had a high altar with vessels of tin, and a picture of no value, also two little side altars." The Government Street Presbyterian Church, Christ Church, and the Cathedral Basilica of the Immaculate Conception, all completed between the late 1830s and the early 1850s, soon became iconic landmarks in the city skyline. Their facades, designed in classical styles by accomplished professional architects, drew the attention of guests, who remembered them as some of the most distinguished architecture in the city. Those who entered these churches could be effusive with their praise. One visitor described the interior of the Presbyterian church, for example, as "altogether the most strikingly beautiful I ever remember to have seen." Others referred to the sanctuaries of the churches as "large and handsome."[24]

The congregations that worshipped in Mobile's churches came in for their share of comments by visitors, both in regard to their piety and their influence on city society at large. "The godly were in force" in Mobile, remembered one visitor to the city late in the antebellum era, citing the number of churches as evidence. "I have seldom seen a better dressed, and never a better conducted assembly, whilst nothing could be more perfectly democratic," commented another after visiting a Mobile church. The Reverend George

Lewis stated that he "enjoyed much kindness and Christian fellowship in Mobile," where he pronounced there to be "no small Christian zeal, love, and liberality among all denominations." He continued: "There is a wholeheartedness about them... which is more rare amongst those that have been brought up in the faith." Lewis became one of the few visitors who published accounts of Mobile to attend services at a Black congregation. He visited the African Methodist Church for worship services while in town and claimed to have found "not fewer than a thousand blacks present" with a white pastor preaching. "The negroes echoed every sentiment that pleased them by an audible Amen! Or Glory be to thy name! or Truth, Lord!" he recorded, clearly surprised at the emotion on display.[25]

One of the gauges visitors used to determine the extent of congregational influence on a community was its observation of the Sabbath, and several commented on Mobile's customs in that regard. They found significant variances, depending upon when the writer visited. "The Sabbath is very indifferently kept here," remembered one, who noted that "eating houses, groceries, apple stands and many other shops are open on this day." Another found only a few stores open on a Sunday during his stay, adding, "Those that were open, I was told, were the stores of Frenchmen, Spaniards, or Jews." Another recorded that during his visit on a Sunday "the town was quiet, though numbers of idlers were standing at the corners of the streets."[26]

In a more worldly vein, visitors found abundant evidence that Mobile was a literate society that valued the written word and education. As many as four newspapers and other weekly gazettes were published in the city at any one time by the 1830s. The city hosted multiple flourishing bookstores as well. Hodgson described perusing the shelves of a well-stocked and busy bookstore and noted the diversity of recent titles in stock. Even if the owner revealed the practical side of Mobile's readers—he acknowledged he sold ten law books to every fiction or nonfiction title—the city appeared to have as well read a populace as anywhere in antebellum America. Some visitors whose accounts are featured here, such as James Silk Buckingham, had actually gone to the city to deliver academic lectures to large and receptive audiences. Buckingham, a world-traveling journalist, recorded that he spoke about the wonders of Egypt at Mobile's Presbyterian church on multiple nights to audiences of about five hundred each evening. He took special notice of the city's Barton Academy, only about a decade old at the time of his visit and the first true public school in the state of Alabama. In his estimation, "there were few better conducted academies in the Union." The city hosted the first public school system in the state, and during the later antebellum years assumed control of a separate school for Creole children and was home to more than two dozen private academies. Spring Hill College, Alabama's oldest continually operating institution of higher education, opened its doors in 1830, and the Medical College of Alabama opened in 1859 in Mobile.[27]

Mobile claimed its fair share of accomplished writers before the war as well. Alexander B. Meek penned poetry and short stories (*Romantic Passages in Southwestern History*), Octavia LeVert wrote a celebrated European travelogue (*Souvenirs of Travel*), Raphael Semmes composed a famous memoir about his service in the Mexican War (*Service Ashore and Afloat*), a teenage Augusta Jane Evans Wilson had already published two popular novels (*Inez: A Tale of the Alamo* and *Beulah*), and the physician and anthropologist Josiah Nott had gained both fame and notoriety for his expositions on racial origins and distinctions (*Types of Mankind*). A host of other Mobile-based writers attained some degree of regional and even national success during the antebellum period, together contributing to the city's reputation in some circles as a place of talent and refined tastes.[28]

But some of the offhand descriptions of random moments and events that visitors witnessed or struck them as unusual rank as some of the most informative about daily life in the city before the Civil War. William Kingsford, visiting from Canada, found the way local hunters "waged unrelenting war" against alligators during the summer hunting season to be striking, for example. Karl Bernhard, the German duke, noted Mobile had a post office located in a bar, making it a "therefore somewhat lively" local landmark. George Featherstonhaugh, the British geologist, recorded that on a walk through Mobile's streets one evening he heard guitar music carried on the breeze. He hunted for the source and found to his delight the unusual scene of "two Spaniards . . . dancing with much grace and national feeling, whilst about a dozen men and women were looking on and singing." None other than William T. Sherman, visiting the area while briefly stationed at Fort Morgan during his prewar military career, remembered the exceptional hospitality the locals extended to soldiers. "Suffice to say that the ladies of Mobile feeling as they ever do for the desolate state of us woebegone bachelors, took pity upon us and made the gentlemen charter a steamboat to come down to see us; How kind! . . . We were invited on board the boat where they had a band of music, wine refreshments, etc., etc."[29]

Others found in the pages of a local paper evidence of attempts to solve common problems in unusual ways. The editor of the *Mobile Mercantile Advertiser* complained about the lengthy list of subscribers in arrears on their subscriptions and called out in print a customer who had been seen "laughing heartily over a paragraph in the paper of a previous morning, but who had not paid his subscription for two years!" The editor wrote a similar notice informing would-be advertisers that the paper could no longer extend credit to them. "Publishers, like lovers," the editor opined, "are generally supposed to be able to live upon air; but even if we were disposed to try the experiment upon ourselves, we are not willing to make it on our families, or our creditors who are not publishers."[30] Thus, small details became enduring memories and fodder for general characterizations of city life for visitors to antebellum Mobile. Their writings provide us a window into day-to-day life in the city we might not otherwise have.

CHAPTER 7

Slavery and the Enslaved

> Their institution is so thoroughly interwoven with their life and habits that they are fully aware that it forms a part of their existence, and as they feel how much horror slavery inspires in Europeans, they wish at once to explain their position.
> —*Francis and Theresa Pulszky*

> The city, with its intelligence and its enterprise, is a dangerous place for the slave. He acquires knowledge of human rights, by working with others who receive wages when he receives none; who can come and go at their pleasure.
> —*John S. C. Abbott*

The dichotomy of free and enslaved people living side by side in the American South fascinated visitors to antebellum Mobile from outside the region and became the subject of much comment in their writing about time they spent there. Judging from the way they approached the subject, it appears that observing the reality of slavery led them to regard it as one of the primary aspects of Mobile life that merited attention. For the majority of visitors—many of whom hailed from Europe, Canada, or the northern states—who published accounts of their time in the city, simply seeing slavery firsthand was a novel experience. Some approached the practice with condemnation, some with a certain degree of misgiving, and still others with a dispassionate neutrality that accepted slavery as a reality. Regardless of their views of the morality of slavery, all from outside the South or who had spent little time in the southern states found its existence in Mobile to be a hallmark of its society.

The institution of slavery was the underpinning of the commercial activity and dynamic economic growth of antebellum Mobile, and enslaved people were ubiquitous in the city. The enslaved represented about a third of the population at any given time between 1813 and 1861, although slaveholders never accounted for more than about 10 percent of its citizens. But in the larger region with which Mobile was connected economically, culturally, and politically, the enslaved comprised nearly half of the total population and accounted for an even larger percentage of the regional economy. Even if Mobile itself did not rank as the epicenter of forced labor, those who visited the city attempted to make sense of the practice through the lens of what they saw there. Almost all in some manner observed and commented upon the peculiar institution as manifested in Mobile.[1]

Visitors to antebellum Mobile often encountered enslaved people well before arriving in the town, as they were a common sight alongside their owners on the steamboats most took to and from the city. For some travelers, confronting the race-based institution of bondage in such close quarters proved both jarring and illuminating, allowing them a close-up of the hypocrisy of the stated ideals of self-determination in America and the lengths to which its people sometimes went to control the lives of so many other people. Nothing shocked these tourists more than the intermingling of white and Black in everyday life in the South. The British botanist Amelia M. Murray, for example, recalled that while she was aboard a steamer bound for Mobile, "a black woman came and sat down by me in the stern of the vessel." This surprised her, as she acknowledged that, from what she had heard of slavery in England, "I imagined negroes were kept at a distance. That is the case in the Northern States, but in the South they are at your elbow everywhere, and always seek conversation." First-time visitors like Murray seemed to find the ubiquitous presence of enslaved people in the South a somewhat unexpected and uncomfortable development. Perhaps these tourists had imagined the enslaved as toiling only in rural cotton fields and not walking along city streets, frequenting business establishments, and traveling on public transportation. The reality of the situation, though, only highlighted the self-serving and purely racial justifications that were the basis of the system of bondage.[2]

Visitors struggled to comprehend the rules of southern social etiquette when they found themselves rubbing elbows with enslaved people—some attempted to engage in awkward conversation and some kept their distance, unsure what level of familiarity was acceptable. Murray struck up a conversation with an enslaved woman aboard the boat she took to Mobile; the elderly and "very communicative" woman told Murray she had a "young mistress in Texas" of whom she professed to be fond. According to what she told Murray, in her youth the woman had sometimes thought "'twould be a

Charity Anderson, whose photograph was taken in Mobile in 1937 as the Works Progress Administration was assembling the Slave Narrative Collection and taking other oral histories, grew up along the Alabama River, where she was enslaved by a tavern owner who also supplied wood to passing steamers. Courtesy of the Library of Congress.

fine thing to be free," but in her mature years had decided she did not think "'twould be mighty fine at all," professing to have "everything I want in the wide world, 'cept jewelry, and that I don't want at all now." It is sometimes difficult for us today to determine exact meanings of conversations recorded in centuries past, but it is likely that the woman told Murray a combination of truths about herself and a few things she thought Murray wanted to hear. Murray wrote of hearing during her trip that an enslaved man had been freed after decades of service and that he had expressed a desire to return to Africa, where he had been kidnapped as a child. Even this manifestation of self-determination came with a note of appreciation for current circumstances, however, as he, according to Murray, wanted to make sure people knew of his gratitude for the education he had received during his years of bondage.

Studio portrait, ca. 1850, of a man enslaved by the Bunker family of Mobile. Courtesy of the History Museum of Mobile.

Clearly, the degree of open self-expression accorded enslaved individuals among white society had limits, and they were careful about what they said.[3]

Few visitors to antebellum Mobile who left published accounts of their experiences discussed the enslaved people as individuals even in the casual manner that Murray did. General observations abound in their pages instead, and for the most part they clumsily attempted to characterize the manners and habits of a third of the city's population with a simple phrase or two. John Guy Vassar, for example, wrote condescendingly that "the negro population is well dressed and happy." Others, such as Robert Russell, were even more superficial. "The large slave population renders the suburbs mean and untidy" was his assessment of the impact of enslaved people on life in the city. The few notable exceptions stand out. James D. Davidson of Virginia recorded that in Mobile he came across an enslaved man whom he actually knew from back home. The man had stopped Davidson in the street and the two talked for a few minutes. The narrative does not elaborate on the enslaved man's situation in Mobile, and the short conversation ended with the man's averring that "he would not go back [to Virginia] if his former master would give him his freedom." One wonders about the veracity of such statements, but they help us understand the social dynamics at play in Mobile before the Civil War.[4]

An enslaved woman named Betsy, who attended to Octavia LeVert, ranks as among the enslaved people most mentioned in the published travel narratives. Fredrika Bremer described Betsy as a "clever, handsome mulatto attendant" who appeared just about everywhere LeVert did, and to observers the two seemed to have a close relationship. Yet, as is so often the case in regard to people held in bondage, the travelers recorded almost nothing beyond the basic facts of Betsy's service even after spending multiple hours in LeVert's company. An enslaved woman owned by LeVert's mother was someone else with whom guests in the city came into contact—in her case as something of a curiosity—but the writers passed along almost nothing about her as a person. One writer described the enslaved woman as "a capital old woman, and apparently quite an original, she perfectly remembers [George] Washington, having seen him once driving out in a carriage on some great occasion in full dress." No doubt she had been prompted to retell the story of this encounter for numerous guests, but listeners seemingly deemed her life and times not worth investigating, unworthy of recording, or both.[5]

The Swedish writer Fredrika Bremer wrote extensively about her travels through Europe and America. Her letters to her sister Agathe, written during a visit to North America from 1849 to 1851, were later published in a two-volume set entitled *Homes in the New World*.

Visitors to Mobile before the Civil War would have seen many enslaved people wherever they ventured in the city. Whether the enslaved were working in the homes of the wealthy, attending public functions in segregated seating, engaged in building or maintenance projects, or running errands for owners, they were part and parcel of the city's antebellum social scene. Some of the enslaved people whom visitors encountered on the streets may have been hired out to work as steamboat hands, stevedores, and dock laborers, and in a variety of types of construction. Slave hiring proved to be a lucrative enterprise for many owners, as it brought them hundreds of dollars per year and usually saved them much of the costs associated with food, housing, and even clothing for bondsmen. Being hired out afforded the enslaved person a certain degree of autonomy that they did not have as part of a plantation gang or as a domestic servant. By some estimates, in 1860 owners were hiring out as many as a thousand enslaved workers, who were living apart from their owners in Mobile in quarters rented by employers. City officials struggled to regulate the practice, as some among the white population feared that enslaved people living out of owners' sight could not be sufficiently controlled and would set a bad example for others. Yet despite the freedom hiring-out offered the enslaved—and the competition they provided to white workers in a variety of trades—the practice grew more common as the years progressed and costs to employers for their labor increased. Still, published visitor accounts made little mention of the practice of hiring the enslaved, perhaps in part because few who observed the enslaved workers packing cotton at the city's port facilities or constructing homes and businesses along its streets fully understood the economics of their situation.[6]

One tourist in pre–Civil War Mobile, Dr. Thomas Nichols of New Hampshire, had a firsthand encounter with the realities of the hiring-out system, however. His host owned some people who had been bequeathed to the man's granddaughter, and he had hired them out to a brickmaking establishment south of the city. The grandfather professed to have great apprehension about their treatment so far from his observation and wanted to make regular checks on them. Nichols accompanied him on one such trip and noted that the man brought the enslaved people "some little comforts, tea, coffee, and tobacco" and inquired about their duties and working conditions. Another visitor, John S. C. Abbott, a native of New England, in straightforward

A residency permit dated April 1, 1859, for an enslaved woman named Mary Ann. It documents that she had permission to live away from the premises of her owner. Courtesy of the History Museum of Mobile.

fashion expressed the inherent threat that hiring out posed to the enslaved and the peculiar institution in which they were ensnared: "The city, with its intelligence and its enterprise, is a dangerous place for the slave. He acquires knowledge of human rights, by working with others who receive wages when he receives none; who can come and go at their pleasure."[7]

While few visitors to antebellum Mobile seemed moved to write in much detail about the economics of slavery or the practicality of hiring out enslaved workers, several sought opportunities to learn about their treatment. Quick, public encounters with the enslaved population gave the tourists little chance for thorough investigations, but visitors took note of every fact they gleaned about the owner-slave relationship while in the city. While en route to Mobile aboard a steamboat, Abbott had an unwelcome occasion to learn about the worst treatment of the enslaved. He recalled that a loud and drunken young man boarded the boat, bragging that he intended to go to Mobile "for a bust," a self-styled vacation that he clearly relished, for he professed to Abbott that "I never expect to get nearer to heaven than I am when I get to Mobile." The unashamed reference to a drunken bender took Abbott aback, but the man's promises regarding his intentions for dealing with the enslaved workers he had left on his plantation shocked Abbott even more. The man swore he would beat his bondsmen severely when he returned if they had not labored to his satisfaction. At that moment Abbott realized the true plight of the enslaved worker, for he knew that they had no chance of working to the owner's satisfaction. The young drunk was the lord of "a remote plantation which no eye of civilization ever sees . . . [so] their doom is one which it is awful to contemplate." Abbott asserted that the "good men at the South abhor" such behavior, but he thought the only way to end such outrages would be "by abolishing the system which legalizes them." While another visitor claimed to have witnessed "no mal-treatment of slaves" while in Alabama or Mobile (one wonders what his definition of proper treatment was), he acknowledged that he did notice that "drunkenness prevails to such a degree among their owners, that I cannot doubt that the power they exercise must often be fearfully abused."[8]

These comments were nothing more than informed speculation, the result of writers' taking at face value the boasting of a drunken man or a projection of how an owner's public behavior might have affected the lives of the enslaved when no outsider could see what he was doing. But a few observers saw the treatment of the enslaved firsthand and wrote about the brutality that often defined the owner-slave relationship. The "barbarity to the Negro servants," reported Adam Hodgson, the British businessman, "was beyond even what I had anticipated." He noted that during his travels in the South, "you continually hear the lash upon their backs, with language which would shock you." While Hodgson mentions that he had witnessed such lashings while visiting plantations in the region, he does not claim he saw them in Mobile. However, an owner's prerogative to inflict severe physical punishment on enslaved people, regardless of location, was fundamental to the institution. The German duke Karl Bernhard recounted seeing a public whipping post near the Mobile city jail. "It was constructed like a sash frame," he wrote. "The lower board on which the feet of the unfortunate being were to stand, could be pushed up or down, to accommodate the height of the individual. Upon it is a block, through which the legs are passed. The neck and arms are passed through another." With evidence such as this, it would have been easy for someone arriving in Mobile for the first time to believe the comment of the Scottish baker who struck up a conversation about slavery with the writer Thomas Hamilton. The baker claimed that "men are treated in this country far worse than brute beasts in Scotland." Such comments would have made it easier to believe the stories that floated on the streets about the cruelty visited upon the enslaved. During his visit to Mobile, the Reverend George Lewis wrote, he had learned that an enslaved man who had escaped was killed by his owner, who made the murder look like an accident.[9]

Notices in the pages of Mobile's newspapers or listening to conversations on the city's streets would have told travelers how frequently the enslaved attempted to escape and how relentlessly the owners pursued them. Notices for runaway slaves were ubiquitous in regional newspapers. Locals posted some of those that appeared in Mobile publications, but many were placed by owners from the interior of Alabama and Mississippi who speculated their bondsmen might have fled to the city. These notices often delineated in minute detail the distinguishing features of enslaved individuals so that they could be identified and captured. Manners of speech, habits, personality traits, and descriptions of height, build, and complexion revealed the level of familiarity between enslavers and the enslaved. But notices that mentioned such details as scars from whippings or cropped ears from other punishments or that the escapee was wearing an iron collar with the owner's name stamped on it—and such notices did appear in Mobile—exposed the brutal discipline exercised on those most desperate for freedom. How all this informed visitors' opinions of Mobile society we can only guess, for few commented much on this particular aspect of slavery during their stays in the city.[10]

A few, though, recorded poignant evidence of just how determined some of the enslaved people were to find freedom, risking life and limb despite the odds stacked against them. One traveler mentioned meeting a man in Mobile who had come to the city seeking legal counsel after one of his enslaved people had died after running away and being captured. The enslaved man had fled aboard a steamboat en route from Montgomery to Mobile. The escapee had been captured and taken back to Montgomery, but before the owner

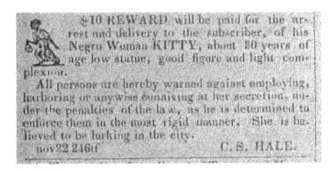

Notices of reward for the capture of runaway slaves that appeared in Mobile newspapers in the 1840s. Courtesy of The Doy Leale McCall Rare Book and Manuscript Library, University of South Alabama.

could reclaim him, he had died of exposure and malnourishment while in the custody of his captors. Another visitor noted that he had heard of an enslaved boy who had been taught to read and write and promised eventual freedom. Apparently his parents were already free and were living in the North, and he fled to be with them, heedless of the daunting journey and likelihood he would be caught. Another tourist ventured past the city jail during his stay and found powerful physical evidence of the force that owners and governmental authorities exerted in attempting to control and punish the behavior of the enslaved. The visitor noticed that the jail was holding several runaway slaves and hanging on a wall were "a huge whip, handcuffs and a number of other irons." Mobile might not have featured the huge cotton plantations where the majority of enslaved people toiled in antebellum Alabama, but the city was no less a participant in the institution in a variety of unsavory ways.[11]

Perhaps the most jarring reminder of Mobile's involvement with the institution of slavery lay in the sordid spectacle of people who were being bought and sold. Mobile served as a primary regional slave market throughout the antebellum period, ranking as perhaps Alabama's largest until Montgomery supplanted it in the 1840s. Still, the volume of slave sales taking place in the city was substantial in the 1840s and 1850s. The main slave market in the city stood on the west side of Royal Street between St. Louis and St. Anthony Streets. A three-story barracks with barred windows during its period of peak activity, the facility served as the epicenter of the repellant trade. Mobile residents were less than eager to show such a facility to their guests, and only a few visitors who subsequently wrote about Mobile mention it with any specificity. Bremer was one of the few to chronicle with any detail her visit to the facility, which she wanted to see out of curiosity. She said little about the conditions in which people lived there, though, mentioning only her encounter with "a few mulatto girls, who remained unsold . . . and who proposed to me that I should purchase them." Perhaps the girls believed that being purchased by a woman might be the best fate they could wish for. All that is certain is that the inspection of enslaved individuals by potential buyers was often reciprocated. Two visitors to Mobile whose written accounts inform this book, Charles H. Russell and Bishop Henry Whipple, left heart-rending narratives of witnessing slave sales that reveal the brutality of the system.[12]

This depiction of an auctioneer soliciting bids for an enslaved man in a typical southern market would have been representative of what visitors to Mobile's slave market might have beheld. Courtesy of the Library of Congress.

"The day before I left Mobile I witnessed a negro sale by auction," wrote Russell. "It was to me a painful sight, but people familiarized to this sight appear to regard it with no more feeling than we do the sale of horses." Russell wrote that he saw a series of men, women, and children brought to the auction block, "well dressed and made clean, and shown to the best advantage." One the auctioneers "represented [a man] as a first rate hand, a good rough carpenter, and warranted sound," a second with "one leg shorter than the other, but warranted sound," and a third described as a "stout full-sized negro, apparently very strong." Russell watched as a boy of perhaps ten years old was sold, and "the big tears rolled down his cheeks . . . notwithstanding the sheriff's caution to him not to cry." Russell also witnessed the auctioneer's calling for bids on "a fine-looking, well-dressed, young mulatto girl, with a child three years old," advertised as "good at sewing and can make shirts." According to Russell, "She appeared to show much anxiety about her fate and when struck off [led away] manifested disappointment and began crying."[13]

Whipple's depiction of the slave sale he witnessed is similarly moving and enlightening. He had a rare opportunity to speak with a few enslaved people before they were placed on the auction block. Had he any doubt of the lack of self-determination among the slave population, they removed it for him. One remarked that he desired to go to Africa for economic freedom since in his estimation only white people could make money in America, while another promised not to work if the sale separated him from his wife. Whipple did not specify the circumstances of the event, but it may have been an estate sale involving many people who had lived and worked together in one place for most of their lives. He noted that "as but few of them had ever been sold, they all appeared to be laboring under the greatest anxiety as to the future." He continued, "When the sale commenced, you could see the negro offered for sale show the greatest anxiety." They as a group displayed obvious signs of mortal fear and visceral dread, which must have been difficult to watch—"the quivering lip, the convulsive twitching of the face, the suppressed tear, the heavy sigh, and the broken answer in reply to different interrogators." Whipple excused slaveholders from the inhumanity of the scene by blaming "speculators who care not how they sell negroes, provided they realize the most money." The pastor also attempted to contrast the speculators with owners who he believed cared for their bondsmen, but he decried the behavior of dealers who "feel no personal interest in the slaves ... and therefore to them they are only a commodity by which they can make money." Despite the revulsion Whipple articulated at seeing signs casually advertising for sale at auction "Slaves, Horses, and Other Property" at certain establishments in the South, he seemingly forgot that all the enslaved people he watched being sold were being bought by other slaveowners. His candid observations, tinted as they were by a blindness to the totality of the reality he witnessed, help us understand one of the most sordid but routine events in Mobile.[14]

By the time Russell and Whipple made their way to Mobile's slave market, southerners had become well versed in the convoluted justifications for holding Black people in bondage. The city's white population proved as adept as any in the region at attempting to exonerate themselves from the stigma of

Slavery and the Enslaved   111

These manifests list the names of slaves being transported on ships entering and leaving the Mobile harbor in the antebellum period. Courtesy of the National Archives.

Notices for slave sales that appeared in Mobile newspapers in the 1840s. Courtesy of The Doy Leale McCall Rare Book and Manuscript Library, University of South Alabama.

the peculiar institution. Travelers revealed that Mobile's citizenry were not shy about discussing slavery, in fact "niggers and cotton—cotton and niggers" became the substance of many conversations, according to one visitor. But in all these discussions they tended to rationalize or vindicate their involvement in the practice. One set of visitors, the Hungarian natives Francis and Theresa Pulszky, remembered being a little taken aback by the way some among the slaveholding class jumped right into a potentially uncomfortable topic at the first opportunity. As they were dining with the wife of Philip Phillips, a lawyer and member of the Alabama legislature, the sisters noted that "in the very first moment of our acquaintance she began to speak about slavery." It was not the first time they had found themselves in such a situation. In their experience in the South, they had found that "people seek this topic with foreigners. Their institution is so thoroughly interwoven with their life and habits that they are fully aware that it forms a part of their existence, and as they feel how much horror slavery inspires in Europeans, they wish at once to explain their position." The Pulszkys observed that few southerners wanted to attempt to defend the institution intellectually but rather that "they invariably appeal to the great difficulty of getting on without it."[15]

While in candid conversations some people acknowledged that slavery's "wrong side could not be altogether denied," visitors were stunned that no one apparently was prepared to even contemplate an eventual end to a system that so blatantly contradicted the basic concepts of life and liberty that Americans claimed to hold dear. A few writers professed to have found people in the South "inventing arguments for perpetuating the bondage of an unhappy race." However, according to travelers who reported meeting anyone in Mobile who had reflected upon the morality of human bondage, the locals appear to have characterized the peculiar institution as immutable instead of making any genuine argument for its continuation. One slaveowner encountered by a visitor to Mobile, for example, made a matter-of-fact assessment of social conditions in the South and professed to see no way to change the situation and instead counseled that all should accept it. "We are all in the same boat, and we must sink or swim together," he advised.[16]

A few travelers, however, such as the outspoken James Silk Buckingham, found what he believed to be direct evidence of how thoroughly southerners actively promoted racism to both justify and continue the institution of slavery. Buckingham had obtained a copy of a speech by Mobile's Dr. Josiah Nott and noted that the address was "redolent of the sentiments and opinions of the South, respecting the negro race." Nott ranked as one of the region's preeminent authorities on medical science at the time, but his anthropological philosophies regarding race were grounded in a theory that white and Black people were essentially different species of humanity. Nott's beliefs demonstrate the corrupt thought process of slaveowners who seemed willing to go to any length to justify the institution of slavery. In Buckingham's opinion, Nott advocated the "most obstinate prejudices," and the Englishman was incredulous that Nott, as a professional, would make such arguments. Permanent residents of the South who had their qualms about the practice usually learned to keep their opinions to themselves or were forced to leave the region, but visitors exposed to the prevailing mental calculus of the white South could sometimes pose the uncomfortable questions that residents dared not ask. When Buckingham, en route to Mobile, invited people to convince him that enslaved people were better off than free whites because they had no cares to worry them, he retorted by asking sarcastically whether they "would like to similarly be released from cares."[17]

A traveler named John Morris who visited Mobile revealed in a dramatic and unusually detailed account how an enslaved person's destiny could rest on the whims of sometimes unprincipled men. During visits to one of the city's gambling houses during a long stay, Morris wrote that he got to know a young servant named William whom he described as "a bright mulatto, about twenty-two years of age, and exceedingly intelligent." A slave trader named George Kent owned William. Morris characterized Kent, as Morris did other slave traders he had met, as "ignorant, cruel, uncouth, and overbearing." While William appeared "attentive and respectful to every one with whom he was thrown in contact," Kent quickly revealed himself as "a most inhuman master, who never spoke a kind word to his slave, or allowed him a moment's pastime.... Frequently for the slightest, and often an imaginary offense, he would take the boy to his sleeping apartment and flog him severely." Morris noted that even Kent's business partner would sometimes "remonstrate with him about his barbarous treatment of the boy" but to little effect. William begged Morris to buy him and take him away from Mobile.[18]

According to Morris, William even offered to help secure the money for his purchase by clandestinely helping Morris beat Kent in a card game. Morris declined but got his associate, a Mr. Forrest, a northern man who had moved to Mobile for business, interested in the scheme. Forrest challenged

The British author, journalist, and politician James Silk Buckingham traveled throughout Europe, North America, and Asia during a long and distinguished career. He earned special attention for his role in journalism in India, having founded a periodical there during a stay of several years. He spent an extended visit to the United States in the late 1830s and early 1840s that formed the basis of his book, *The Slave States of America*. Courtesy of the National Portrait Gallery, London. Attributed to Clara S. Lane.

Kent to a game, staking a few hundred dollars on the outcome. With William standing behind Kent's chair and secretly communicating to Forrest the cards Kent held, the slave trader soon found himself losing the game. At last out of money, he offered William as collateral for a $1,500 bet, convinced he could win his money back from Forrest. He of course still lost , leaving a pile of money, plus William, in Forrest's possession. However, as "nothing at that period created more terror in the mind of the Northerner living in the South than the thought of being in any way implicated in anything like a negro conspiracy," Forrest turned to Morris for assistance. Morris claimed that, after detecting Forrest's intentions to sell William in New Orleans, he ultimately escorted the young man to Ohio and helped him secure his freedom with "the requisite free papers."[19]

It is difficult to know what to make of the running dialogue central to Morris's story, for his account is given with so many supposedly verbatim quotes that it reads more like a work of fiction than a typical travel narrative. Even if Morris embellished some of the details to tell what he believed to be an engrossing story, the entire saga he recounts reveals the capriciousness of some slaveowners and the lengths to which enslaved individuals resorted to improve their lives. Morris's story would have rung true to many visitors who witnessed slavery in Mobile and spent any time critically observing the plight of the enslaved and the attitudes of enslavers. While some travelers simply provided a survey of the city's society, others, like Morris, were moved to condemn human bondage. "I never left a place with more satisfaction," wrote Hodgson, the British businessman, in his account of a stay in Mobile during a tour of the South. As he sailed into the Gulf after spending time in one of the world's most slave-dependent economies, he "could not help reflecting [on] . . . the moral darkness" of the region."[20]

That visitors made so little comment about Mobile's notable free Black population perhaps reveals that these tourists could not or did not distinguish them from the hired-out enslaved people these writers encountered in the city. As a facet of the city's antebellum society, the topic is particularly undeveloped in their narratives. At the time, Mobile's free Black population accounted for about 40 percent of all such Alabama residents and represented the largest such community in the state and anywhere in the region outside of New Orleans., Many were descended from the Creole residents of the region in the colonial era, while a smattering of more recently emancipated bondsmen had remained in the area. The legal protections afforded Black Creoles in Mobile ranked as unique; they were a protected class by long-standing custom and official statements in the terms of the Louisiana Purchase, which were reaffirmed in 1819 in the Adams-Onis Treaty between the United States and Spain.[21]

Free Blacks were a prominent part of antebellum Mobile. They were active in the city's small businesses, including a number of Black merchants who were attempting to carve out a niche in the city's market and others who provided a variety of products and services. The city had a Creole school that also served the free Black community by the 1850s—at a time when fewer than half of all children in the city attended school—and Creoles maintained their own social clubs, civic organizations, and fire companies. This did not mean Mobile's white population ever was entirely comfortable with the situation, however, and officials made occasional efforts to require free Blacks to register with white guardians, which was largely impractical and rarely enforced. Segregated public facilities, such as Ludlow's Theater, which contained boxes for white, Black, and mixed race guests, were a part of the city's public environment. Mobile's sizable free Black community was an anomaly in a slaveholding region, subjected to continual redefinition of its autonomy within the city's larger society. Perhaps visitors staying in the city for only a few days at a time were ill-equipped to paint the full picture of this aspect of Mobile's civic culture and may have been unaware of the size and uniqueness of the free Black community.[22]

Published visitor narratives have left us with only fleeting, undeveloped vignettes that hint at the position of free Blacks in Mobile society. One visitor's experience aboard a steamboat leaving the city poignantly illustrates the unstable status of free Blacks in Mobile. The traveler noticed two free Black women, to whom he referred as mulatto, traveling on the boat with him. Observing that they were neither fully white nor fully Black, he became fascinated with how they negotiated their position aboard the boat. He recorded that they ate last at the table at mealtimes—the first bell called the captain and all white passengers to sit down, the second summoned the pilot, clerk, and all white laborers, stewards, and servants aboard the boat, with the third bell calling Black and mixed race passengers. The free Black women were not allowed to sit with white passengers, but neither were they welcome among the Black laborers and servants. He remembered:

> They had to retire to the pantry, where they took their meals standing. The contrast of their finery in dress and ornament, with the place in which they took their isolated and separate meal, was painfully striking. What rendered it more so, to me at least, was this—that however a man might yearn to break down these barriers which custom and prejudice has raised against a certain race, the exhibition of any such feeling, or the utterance of any such sentiment, would undoubtedly injure the very parties for whom his sympathy might be excited, or on whose behalf it might be expressed.

Obviously, the story of antebellum Mobile's free Black community is woefully incomplete, one that published visitor accounts of life in the city are inadequate to address.[23]

CHAPTER 8

Entertainment and Celebrations

> In nearly every single building along the street facing the river, and also in many of those in the streets leading down to the river could be found a liquor-shop of one kind or another. In many of these places were played heavy percentage games, like chuck, rondo, craps, and similar institutions.
> —*John Morris*

> There were some marvelous processions . . . to celebrate the New Year. These appeared to be representations "of all the world and the rest of mankind" and a little besides. . . . Each had a good large noisy band of music.
> —*Emmeline Stuart Wortley*

Guests in antebellum Mobile took in some of the city's several recreational and entertainment offerings during their stays. These included a number of diversions not available in some of the region's smaller communities, or at least not on the scale Mobile offered. They watched various diversions and special citywide celebrations, and their descriptions of what they saw form one of more intimate windows into life in the city from 1813 to 1861. From trips to the scenic bayfront and attendance at theater productions to whiling away the night hours at grog halls and gambling houses, the amusement possibilities were several and diverse for residents and guests alike. When coupled with the famed Mardi Gras celebrations that began during this period and the city's penchant for rolling out the red carpet for important guests, visitors had abundant opportunities to observe Mobile at its most relaxed and festive.[1]

Short trips to scenic spots along the bay or in the forested low hills beyond town, located south and west of the city respectively, became some of antebellum Mobile's most popular tourist attractions. Each offered different but expansive views of Mobile's natural setting. The magnificent sight of Mobile Bay from Choctaw Point seems to have impressed all who beheld it. Reaching the spot required a ride of two or three miles along a grand avenue that cut through a large magnolia grove and showcased Mobile's lush natural environment. This grove, one visitor wrote, embodied "the great charm, beauty, and attraction of Mobile. The drive... is over an excellent plank road, through the bowery avenues of which are to be attained at every turn most picturesque glimpses over the Bay of Mobile." Another exclaimed, "A beautiful country walk it was; there is nothing equal to it at New Orleans." The British artist Victoria Welby was enraptured by her surroundings on her trip to what many called "the sea-side." She reported, "The trees actually almost dipped into the water" and "were of the most magnificent emerald green I ever saw, towering to the height of more than a hundred feet, and spreading their glossy and luxuriant branches all around." The writer and musician Emmeline Stuart Wortley pronounced the drive through the magnolia forest, with glimpses of the shimmering blue waters of the bay, "unspeakably magnificent." Yet another visitor gushed, "The neighborhood of the town on the seashore is delightful; the air full of fragrance."[2]

A few miles west of town stood another popular natural attraction known as Spring Hill. Accessed by a smooth shell road, this "favourite spot . . . for recreation" was the home of a thriving suburb of small estates positioned on and around an elevated spot offering a commanding view of the countryside. Regarded as healthier than the city itself, given its elevation and clear springs bubbling out of the hillside, Spring Hill early on became, one traveler wrote, "the spot to which the inhabitants of Mobile fly for refuge during the season of yellow fever." Visitors were impressed with the neighborhood's "pretty private residences," and both its built environment and natural setting ranked it as one of the Mobile area's most memorable points of interest.[3]

As for pastimes among Mobile's resident population, guests found that few forms of entertainment enjoyed a wider base of support than the theater. Theaters were a vital part of the city's social scene for both temporary and permanent residents and enjoyed a large and diverse audience in the antebellum city. It speaks to the popularity of theaters that they were one of the few venues other than churches where the city's white and Black populations might attend at the same time, albeit in segregated seating. Mobile hosted a theater as early as the early 1820s, when Noah Ludlow built the first on Royal Street at the intersection of Theatre Street. In short order theaters became mainstays of the city's entertainment offerings, with several in operation at various times before the Civil War. Over the years new ones would be built and older ones remodeled—one theater opened over a billiard parlor in 1832; a small one appeared on Government Street near Barton Academy in 1837; a fifteen-hundred-seat facility (the same size as today's Lunt-Fontanne Theater, one of the largest on Broadway) opened later on St. Emanuel Street. Others came and went, many with short life spans but collectively building an ever-larger audience for the dramatic arts in Mobile and serving as a gathering spot for its residents and visitors.[4]

Most theaters staged productions from approximately November until May to coincide with the city's trading season. Through their doors came full-time residents, brokers and merchants in town during the cotton-trading season, planters and their wives during their winter stays, upcountry newlyweds on their honeymoons, ships' crews and cargo workers, and all manner of other visitors passing through the city. These crowds witnessed perfor-

A Mobile theater, depicted in the margin of Haire and Goodwin's 1824 map of Mobile. Courtesy of the Library of Congress.

mances given by casts ranging from amateurs to some of the leading actors of the day. Shows might be presented only a few times or as many as four to six times a week for a period of eight weeks or more.[5]

Visitors to the city commented on their impressions of the quality of Mobile's theaters and the support they enjoyed. Fredrika Bremer claimed to be impressed with the talent of the cast she saw perform *Jenny Lind in Heidelberg* and *The Daughters of the Stars*, and she attended the theater repeatedly during an extended stay. Bishop Whipple observed that Mobile's theater met with "very good encouragement." His opinion would have been deemed accurate—during most seasons—by the theater owner Sol Smith, who reported that "Mobile, Ala. has at times been one of the best theatrical cities in the United States. . . . The audiences were easily pleased, and the actors exerted themselves to the utmost in their several roles, in gratitude for the leniency of the public." During an age in which rowdy, and at times unruly, gatherings seemed to be more the norm than the exception, Mobile audiences seem to have been for the most part well behaved, according to visitors. For example, John Morris, an Ohio native, expressed relief that, in comparison with some other places he had visited, a "want of decorum was never permitted in the Mobile and New Orleans theaters."[6]

While the numbers of guests gathered in her home were much smaller than those at any of Mobile's theaters, the salon of the socialite Octavia LeVert may have been one of Mobile's most popular venues for elite tourists in the years just before the Civil War. "Madame LeVert," as she came to be known, and her husband, Dr. Henry S. LeVert, lived in a grand house on Government Street, where she hosted social events that were the talk of the town. The granddaughter of a signer of the U.S. Constitution and the daughter of a territorial governor of Florida, LeVert was well traveled, fluent in multiple languages, and had an uncanny ability to be granted an invitation to visit anyone she desired. She corresponded with the likes of Edgar Allan Poe and Washington Irving, and she hosted prominent entertainers and artists, politicians, and other noted guests at her home. Possessed of a disarming down-to-earth charm and an engaging personality, LeVert had an unusual social grace that drew people to her and encouraged conversation. To be welcomed into her parlor was to gain entry into Mobile society, as she was a prominent hostess who seemed to know everybody. "I have also

The Mobile socialite Octavia Walton LeVert, by Thomas Sully. Courtesy of the Historic Mobile Preservation Society.

seen at Mrs. Le V's," remembered one visitor, "a great number of the grandees of Mobile, and more lovely young ladies I have never met with." Attending an event held at LeVert's home, remembered another, ensured one would be afforded an opportunity to meet "just the people you most wish to see." One guest ranked Madame Levert as the "particular attraction of the place—a rare and radiant woman, who embodies and expresses in her charming person the richness, sweetness, brightness, and exuberance of the sunny South." To another she was nothing less than "one of the most delightful people in the world."[7]

A handful of visitors attempted to go beyond their fascination with LeVert herself and describe her gatherings. They described the interior of the house, which was decorated with roses from the garden and well appointed, as at once beautiful and inviting, a poetic abode in the opinion of one guest. Her conversation—"as interesting as it is lively" in the estimation of Francis and Theresa Pulszky—gave the gatherings warmth and light. The subjects of conversation included everything from travel and politics to "Transcendentalists and practical Christians, of Mormonism and Christianity." Those welcomed into this epicenter of Mobile society remembered LeVert as a vital component of their experience in the city, as much a part of the place as "the most delicious breezes and odours of the South, with the verdure of magnolia forests, with the fresh roar of the Mexican Gulf, with the sun and song of birds in the orange groves," Fredrika Bremer wrote.[8]

Public events, such as touring acts and a variety of demonstrations, were popular in pre–Civil War Mobile. For example, during a tour of major cities in 1848, the showman Gardner Quincy Colton staged an exhibition for several weeks in Franklin Hall on St. Joseph Street and the Alhambra on Royal Street. Included among his offerings were a huge mural painting, an explanation of telegraph technology, an artist re-creating some of the world's most famous paintings and sculptures, and demonstrations of the effects of laughing gas (nitrous oxide). Guests gained admission for a mere twenty-five cents for adults, ten cents for children. Hot air balloon demonstrations, boat races, traveling circus acts, animal exhibitions—lions and leopards passed through town on occasion—all added to the amusement opportunities for a growing city along one of the most well-traveled water transportation routes of the era. Other smaller animal curiosities drew the curious as well, such as the baby alligator kept in a tub outside the entrance to a saloon.[9]

Mobile also offered residents and guests several other types of entertainment. A racetrack, cockfighting pits, numerous bars, several gambling dens, and even a few brothels beckoned those with time and money on their hands. Horse racing was popular throughout the South, and the Bascombe Race Course, built in the 1830s and located just outside the city limits, became a regional mecca. Interest in the sport dated to Mobile's earliest days as an American city; the Mobile Jockey Club had formed in 1823. Cockfights, where rowdy crowds placed wagers on the rooster of their choice, were also popular among a certain portion of Mobile society, but few travelers' accounts reflect much awareness of horse racing or cockfighting.[10]

Visitors could not help but notice, however, the numerous watering holes of Mobile and their contribution to the port city's boisterous nightlife. "From dark to dawn, lawlessness stalked abroad rampant in Mobile," wrote one visitor, who claimed that "gangs of drunken boatmen, sailors, and reckless adventurers, staggered through the streets, making night hideous with obscene songs and loud oaths." Another disilluioned visitor reported, "The habits of drinking... are more openly practiced and encouraged in the cities of the South than at the North. Grog-shops of the common order abound." Another reported that he saw in Mobile's streets "many persons the worse for liquor." One traveler sniffed, "In nearly every single building along the street facing the river, and also in many of those in the streets leading down to the river, could be found a liquor-shop of one kind or another. In many of these places were played heavy percentage games, like chuck, rondo, craps, and similar institutions."[11]

Visitors were sometimes astonished at how openly the city's brothels operated; at least one apparently did business in a house with no blinds or curtains and doors that often were left open. The visitor John Morris wrote that in Mobile "lewd women with their more degraded associates drove decency to cover with their abandoned talk and gestures. Boatmen, longshoremen, and sailors, spent among these abandoned harlots their hard earnings, and drank the poisonous fluids which maddened their brains." Summarizing all he had seen, he proclaimed that he doubted "if there could have been found on the face of the globe, a place with even five times its population, where crime, debauchery, and lawlessness of every description, reigned rampant to such a fearful extent."[12]

Of Mobile's nighttime pastimes, gambling drew the most comment from Mobile's visitors, both for the numbers of people engaged in it and the spectacle it presented to those unaccustomed to such attractions. In a number of establishments that made little or no attempt to hide their business despite their technical illegality, patrons played faro, roulette, keno, and even lotteries all through the night. Several factors made Mobile a natural center for gambling activities. A port city with an unusually high number of transient workers and traders—many flush with cash having just been paid for their toil on long voyages—and a large number of other visitors and newcomers in a veritable boom town proved ideal for those providing games of chance. By the 1830s Mobile had become, one visitor wrote, "the favorite gaming place in the South," and it featured a number of establishments with "finely furnished rooms... with carpets, curtains, sideboards, etc.," wherein "all genteel-looking persons were permitted to play." The city's proliferation of fine gambling houses was widely known. "The glowing description which was given me, of the gambling facilities of Mobile, and the immense amount of money in circulation in that city," John Morris recalled, "induced me to take a lake-boat and visit that place." He noted that some establishments provided guests with "gratuitous dinners and suppers" as an inducement to try their hand at games, and the action continued until daylight. "With but little to intimidate them," Bishop Whipple wrote, on display were "the first specimens of gaming which is so fashionable throughout the western world." One visitor claimed to have counted more than forty faro games and three dozen roulette wheels, all doing "a flourishing business" during his visit.[13]

The epicenter of antebellum Mobile's gambling scene was in a block in the city's business district of multistory buildings known as Shakespeare's Row. Its origins are a bit hazy, but by the 1840s the Spanish-style building complex, with a large shared courtyard and multiple gateways on the surrounding streets, contained more than two dozen gaming rooms. Morris left the most colorful description of the place after conducting a thorough examination of its interior. Though he frequented the place voluntarily, he scorned the facility as "one vast gambling-hell... [where] from early candle-light till the break of day, the rattling of faro-checks and the spinning of roulette-wheels could be heard without cessation."[14]

Other diversions, such as the appearance in town of famous people, were occasions for the whole city to join in days of celebration while many of the normal rhythms of day-to-day life came to a temporary halt. These events gave Mobile a chance to preen and throw some of its largest parties. Perhaps no visit during the antebellum era caused quite as much of a stir as the visit by the Marquis de Lafayette in February 1825 during his famous tour of the

United States. The nation feted him as a hero, both for what he had done—the military leader was a friend of George Washington's, and they had fought side by side during the Revolutionary War—and for what he was, one of the last noted figures from the storied founding era. In some ways, Lafayette's arrival in Mobile marked a symbolic transformation of the up-and-coming city from a rude and recently acquired American backwater to a cosmopolitan center. It put the city in the nation's consciousness however briefly and gave it its first significant opportunity to demonstrate its sophistication. Lafayette's visit also became one of the most carefully documented appearances of a famous person in town, one that residents at the time would think of as a defining event in Mobile's history. Huge crowds turned out for a welcome that included a formal reception and a grand ball that threw the community "into great excitement and hilarity," according to one observer.[15]

The general arrived on a riverboat after multiple stops in eastern, central, and southwestern Alabama. A cannonade, crowds, and an appointed committee greeted his boat. The delegation escorted him to the center of town where he found "a triumphal arch, the four corners of which were ornamented with the flags of Mexico, the Republics of South America and Greece, and in the middle was raised that of the United States." Dignitaries then took Lafayette to a large hall "constructed for his reception, where he found all the ladies, to whom he was introduced." Lafayette gave a speech in which he discussed Mobile's colonial rule by the French, British, and Spanish and the blessings of liberty ultimately provided by the patriots who had won America's independence from Great Britain. Afterward he attended the grand ball, where he chose to chat with locals rather than dance on his only night in the city. According to legend that generations clung to tenaciously, Lafayette remarked during the evening that Mobile contained the fairest women in all of America. Despite the several days of activities that Mobilians had planned for him, he left for New Orleans the next morning in order to keep to his packed schedule. Crowds again thronged the wharf to see him off.[16]

Visits by other prominent people, while not accompanied by quite the fanfare of Lafayette's appearance, were nonetheless big events in the city's social life. The former presidents Martin Van Buren and Millard Fillmore stayed in Mobile in the 1840s and 1850s, as did Henry Clay, the former House Speaker, senator, and secretary of state, and John C. Calhoun, the vice president from 1825 to 1832. Their visits served as a sort of confirmation of the town's growing position of regional prominence, and they, too, received elaborate welcomes. The pomp accompanying the arrival of former president James K. Polk in mid-March 1849, only a few weeks after his term of office had ended, demonstrated how seriously the city was committed to marking such occasions.[17]

Polk himself provided the best account of his short stay in Mobile, recording in his diary his experience and, by extension, a little of life in the town. Polk wrote that he reached the Mobile area aboard a steamer on the morning of March 19, 1849, whereupon he was met by another boat with a crowd of citizens and a local delegation sent to greet him. "The two boats were soon lashed," Polk remembered, "one on each side of the *Emperor*, on which I was." Before the former president and his entourage could reach the dock, however, yet another steamer, also loaded with well-wishers, joined the parade into port. Polk beheld the throng that had come out to welcome him, remarking

Former president James K. Polk visited Mobile in 1849. Courtesy of the Library of Congress.

that the wharf seemed to be "covered with people." An additional "large concourse of people of both sexes were on shore." Hailed with salutes fired from artillery aboard boats and on shore, Polk disembarked and made his way to a hotel, where the mayor and other city officials provided an official welcome. Polk was feted with a dinner and flattered with even more visitors and gushing introductions. Not until later in the day did he have an opportunity to explore the city with a small group of confidants and hosts during a ride to "the hospitable mansion of Col. Philips." After enjoying tea, he went to the theater. Those inside welcomed Polk with thunderous applause "and every demonstration of respect." So "exceedingly fatigued and exhausted" was he (he died of exhaustion only months later) that he did not stay until the end of the performance. The statesman pronounced the entire experience "most imposing and magnificent," and it was indeed a demonstration of the enthusiasm and lavishness with which the city embraced notable guests.[18]

Mobilians did not need a visit by a noted individual to throw a party, however. The theater owner Noah Ludlow remembered a number of large parties and banquets during the "very joyous" winter of 1824–25 when he staged plays in the town, including one commemorating the inauguration of John Quincy Adams as president. Mobilians regularly held balls on the birthday of George Washington, Fourth of July revelries, and raucous celebrations of the anniversary of the Battle of New Orleans (January 8) featuring food, music, dancing, and militia drills. All were mainstays of the city's events calendar. "The military of Mobile were out today," noted one visitor, who happened to be in town during one of these special exhibitions. "It was a grand gala day with them and they made a fine show, the uniforms and equipage was in good taste and in good order and they drilled very well." Even somewhat ordinary occurrences, such as an election day, could lead to a party. James Silk Buckingham, visiting the city during a mayoral election, wrote that he saw so much drunkenness in the streets that he believed himself "bound to say that . . . worse would, perhaps, be impossible."[19]

Mobile's most iconic celebrations, though, were those associated with the secret mystic societies whose members paraded masked through the streets in celebration of Mardi Gras. These public spectacles, featuring fancifully decorated floats, were revived in 1830 as a reprise of an old French tradition begun in 1703 by the French at the first settlement of Mobile. Between 1830 and

1861 these parades customarily took place on New Year's Eve. A Pennsylvania-born businessman named Michael Kraft is credited with reviving interest in the tradition after establishing the first of Mobile's mystic societies, the legendary Cowbellion de Rakin Society, in 1830. Equipped with hoes, rakes, and cowbells, and no doubt animated by a dose of liquid spirits, the group danced through city streets. By the 1840s several similar groups were active in the city and added horse-drawn floats to the festivities. The popularity and form of the celebration was exported to New Orleans in the 1850s and taken up with gusto. With names such as the Strikers Independent Society, the Rising Generation, the Indescribables, and the Tea Drinkers Society, these Mobile organizations laid the enduring cornerstone of city carnival society. To visitors in the years before the Civil War who got to witness Mobile's Mardi Gras revelry, the spectacle ranked as memorable indeed.[20]

Dating to just before and after the Civil War, these ornately embellished invitations to balls thrown by the Cowbellion de Rakin Society and Strikers Independent Society hint at the pomp that accompanied Mardi Gras festivities in the mid-nineteenth century. Left: courtesy of Historic Mobile Preservation Society. Right: courtesy of the Mobile Carnival Museum.

Victoria Welby remembered that on New Year's Eve "several Chinese processions passed by," probably costumed whites, brandishing "coloured paper-lamps" and were "accompanied by bands of rather a questionable excellence." She continued: "There was also another procession, which I believe was intended to represent the different inhabitants of Olympus, drawn by various four-footed inhabitants of the earth." Wortley noted that during her stay in Mobile she saw "some marvelous processions . . . to celebrate the New Year. These appeared to be representations 'of all the world and the rest of mankind' and a little besides. Olympus was there," she added, along with "pig-tailed Mandarins, pagodas, and colored lanterns on poles," juxtaposed with "tridents, chariots, and mythological divinities." Accompanying all the groups was "a good large noisy band of music," with the players of the horns "distending their cheeks almost to bursting," and "the drums were beaten till they were quite beat." During the Cowbellion's twenty-first anniversary parade, a reporter wrote that members "brought out this time about seventy of the different characters of Shakespeare" for a torchlight march. "Another company, called the Strikers . . . also appeared . . . representing, in dress and figure, many of the heroes of antiquity; at both places dancing and merriment closed the scene." According to the reporter, "The whole town seemed turned out for a frolic."[21]

Of course not every Mobilian attended the theater, gambled in the city's dens, or lined the streets for Mardi Gras parades. Neither did every visitor demonstrate an awareness of the existence of such pastimes—some may have thought them not worth mentioning or may not have been aware of them in their totality because of the timing and circumstances of their visit. But in visitors' eyes, the existence of such opportunities for diversion and merriment helped distinguish the city from other communities, and their accounts of what they saw, participated in, or heard about form a unique window into the reality of life in the city during this period.

Afterword

While Mobile saw a remarkable degree of continuity of life for much of the Civil War, Alabama's secession from the Union in January 1861 marked the beginning of a new and different era in the city's history. Politically, socially, economically, and even to some degree physically, the war years would mark the turbulent end of one period and the dawning of another. That story, a four-year saga featuring revelry and sorrow, bustle and bust, parties and preparation for invasion, defiance and surrender, comprise a chapter as important in the city's rich history as its colonial experience.

The long-ago sights, sounds, and smells of Mobile's antebellum period have largely vanished, but a few spots remain that provide fleeting glimpses of it. What follows is a discussion of a few spots in and around modern Mobile where a visitor might grasp some bit of the city as it existed during the era discussed in this book. I am not offering a comprehensive antebellum tour guide by any measure and instead suggest a few public points of interest evocative of a distant past that may stir the imagination of those seeking to learn about it.

To get a sense of Mobile's maritime past and the timelessness of its distinct natural environment the first place to visit is **Cooper Riverside Park** (101 S. Water Street). One of the few public spaces for accessing the city's namesake river, the park connects the Outlaw Convention Center and the GulfQuest Maritime Museum. The Mobile River's might and majesty are on full display here, and the surrounding commotion of dry docks and cargo-loading facilities, and the constant coming and going of tugs, container ships, and barges, drive home the point that today Mobile still has one of the nation's busiest ports. Despite the proliferation of modern development, it is easy to imagine the steamers that once churned the river's rolling waters and antebellum visitors stepping ashore on one of the dozens of wooden docks that once lined more than a mile of riverfront. Most arriving by water would have been coming from the north, descending the Tombigbee and Alabama River systems and journeying down the Mobile. Some returned along the same route, while others continued south, into the waters of Mobile Bay and out into the open ocean about thirty miles away.

Two streets to the west of the park is **Royal Street**, a primary commercial thoroughfare before the Civil War and still a vital part of the city's business sector today. A trip along the street is studded with reminders of Mobile's antebellum past and takes the visitor past several locations that figured prominently in explorations of the city by the travelers whose accounts are featured in this book. South of the street's intersection with Government Street, Royal Street passes the **old city hall and marketplace, now the History Museum of Mobile** (111 S. Royal Street); the reconstruction of Fort Conde (150 S. Royal Street), the original of which was built by the French in the early 1700s; and the only remaining ruins of the original fort, adjacent to Mardi Gras Park (163 Government Street). On the opposite side of the park stands the venerable **Christ Church Cathedral** (115 S. Conception Street), opened in 1840. On the south side of the reconstruction of Fort Conde, along Theatre Street, is the **Conde-Charlotte House** (104 Theatre Street). The house-museum interprets multiple periods of Mobile's colonial and American eras; elements of the structure date to the 1820s, and most of its facade dates to the late 1840s. North of Government Street, modern Royal Street is the home of some of the downtown area's largest hotels, including the famous **Battle House** (26 N. Royal Street). The current structure here dates to the early 1900s, but it stands on the spot of its noted predecessor. Just north of the Battle House, between St. Louis and St. Anthony Streets, is a historic marker at the former site of Mobile's primary **slave market**.

Continuing up Royal Street, crossing St. Anthony Street, and taking a left after crossing Conception Street takes the visitor into the **De Tonti Square Historic District**. This nine-block area, roughly bounded by Adams Street on the north, Claiborne Street on the west, St. Anthony Street on the south, and Conception Street on the east, contains dozens of antebellum homes built in the Federal, Greek Revival, and Italianate styles. Between 1840 and 1860 it was one of Mobile's wealthiest neighborhoods, showcasing the affluence of its rising merchant class and the city's growing economic influence in the region. Many of the visitors on whose accounts this book is based walked these streets and commented on the opulence of the homes they found here. The Italianate **Richards-DAR House** (256 N. Joachim Street), completed in 1860 for the steamboat captain Charles G. Richards, is operated as a museum by the city's chapters of the Daughters of the American Revolution.

The Richards-DAR House, completed in 1860. Courtesy of the author.

Turning south again for a few blocks along St. Joseph Street, which parallels Royal Street one block to the west, will take the visitor past **Bienville Square**. A central gathering spot in the city for generations, the park is named for the city's founder, Jean-Baptiste Le Moyne, Sieur de Bienville. Its use as a public space dates to the 1820s, but its establishment as a park with its current borders dates to about 1850. The square, with its live oaks, memorials, and central fountain, postdates the antebellum era but is nonetheless evocative of the green spaces visitors would have encountered in the city before the war. Today the square is a quiet spot amid the bustle at the heart of downtown. Running along the south side of the park is Dauphin Street (one way west to east in this area), one of the most iconic streets in Mobile. Connecting the commercial waterfront with city's suburbs to the west, this original city street is today well known to visitors for its concentration of restaurants, bars, candy shops, and galleries. Several of these businesses are located in historic storefronts dating to the antebellum period.

Cathedral-Basilica of the Immaculate Conception, completed in the 1850s. Courtesy of the author.

Cathedral Square and the Cathedral-Basilica of the Immaculate Conception stand on either side of Claiborne Street, which intersects Dauphin Street three blocks west of Bienville Square. Construction of the majestic cathedral, one of Mobile's most elegant architectural gems, began in the early 1830s on the site of an earlier wooden cathedral but was not completed until 1850 because of financial setbacks. The square across the street from it served as a cemetery for the Catholic church in the colonial period and later became the site of several commercial buildings. These were cleared away in the 1970s to create a green space that today is used for community events. The **Bishop Portier House** (307 Conti Street), built in the 1830s, is on Conti Street on the south side of Cathedral Square. The home is named for its original owner, Bishop Michael Portier, and is recognized as one of Mobile's best examples of Creole cottage architecture.

One block to the south is **Government Street**. A primary east-west thoroughfare since the antebellum era, the route dates to the earliest days of Mobile's Spanish period. It received its name for the concentration of government facilities that lined it. The name is still appropriate, as the municipal government complex, main branch of the city library, and several other city and federal offices are located on the street. In the years before the Civil War, the road ran only a short distance past the city limit. Still, visitors recognized Government Street as one of the most distinguished in the city for both its width and the many large homes and public facilities that, shaded by the canopy of a forest, flanked the road. Some of the city's most celebrated structures of the antebellum era still stand along this venerable promenade, including two nationally significant Greek Revival structures, **Government Street Presbyterian Church** (300 Government Street) and **Barton Academy** (504 Government Street). The church, a stunning example of Greek Revival architecture, was completed in 1837. Barton Academy, home to the first public school in the state of Alabama, opened in 1839. Farther west along Government Street is the **Raphael Semmes House** (804 Government Street), built in the 1850s by Peter Horta but known by its association with the Confederate naval captain and commerce raider who spent the final years of his life here. Behind the Ben May Public Library and the Mobile Local History and Genealogy Library just a block to the southeast lies the **Church Street Graveyard** (106 South Scott Street). Mobile's oldest public cemetery, it dates to the early statehood period and contains more than a thousand burials, many marked with some of the city's most noted examples of funerary art.

By proceeding west on Government Street, taking a left onto George Street, and following the signs, the visitor will find the **Historic Oakleigh Complex** (350 Oakleigh Place). The complex features one of Mobile's most prominent house museums, built in the 1830s by the cotton broker and merchant James Roper in what was then the countryside just beyond the city limits. The house is an excellent example of the type of suburban estate visitors to antebellum Mobile would have encountered in their travels. Also located within the Oakleigh complex are the Cox-Deasy Cottage (1850), used as a barracks by federal troops after the Civil War, and the Historic Mobile Preservation Society's Minnie Mitchell Archives—a treasure trove

One of Mobile's iconic historic homes, Oakleigh stood outside the city limits when originally built. Today it is a museum. Photograph by the author.

of local historical records collected by the society for decades. A few blocks to the south is **Magnolia Cemetery** (1202 Virginia Street), the final resting place for generations of Mobilians, including many of its antebellum-era residents. The cemetery opened in 1836 and contains more than 120,000 burials. The easiest way to reach the cemetery from Oakleigh is by returning to Government Street and taking a left on Ann Street.

Several blocks to the north, along **Springhill Avenue** and located about a half mile from each other are two public facilities that showcase the changes in Mobile's high-style architecture during the antebellum period. The homes are outstanding examples of the type of residential construction visitors to Mobile would have seen and commented upon during their stays. The **Vincent-Doan House**, built in the 1820s in the French Creole style and recognized as one of the oldest homes in Mobile, today houses the Mobile Medical Museum (1664 Springhill Avenue). Captain Benjamin Vincent built the house as a secondary residence that he and his family used to escape the heart of the city in the warm months, when epidemics of yellow fever were most likely. A short distance to the west is the **Bragg-Mitchell Mansion** (1906 Springhill Avenue). Judge John Bragg, brother of the Confederate general Braxton

Bragg, completed the structure, one of the city's most opulent antebellum homes, in 1855.

To the west of downtown lies the **Spring Hill neighborhood**, which during the antebellum era was a suburb separated from the town proper by a few miles of forest. To reach the general area of elevation for which the neighborhood is named—an incline as much as two hundred feet above sea level (downtown Mobile lies at a mere ten feet) in the otherwise flat Gulf Coastal Plain—visitors should drive west along Springhill Avenue, Dauphin Street, and Old Shell Road. The Spring Hill area contains several private antebellum homes and hosts Spring Hill College (4000 Dauphin Street). While little remains of the original 1830s college campus, **Stewartfield** (4307 Old Shell Road), a Greek Revival home dating to 1849, stands on the edge of the campus at the end of a live oak–lined driveway known as the Avenue of the Oaks. Today the college uses the house as an event center. Its circular drive is the last vestige of what was a racetrack during the antebellum period.

Returning to downtown and picking up Government Street, then taking a right onto Claiborne Street will take the visitor past the **Phoenix Fire Museum** (203 S. Claiborne Street). It showcases the history of Mobile's volunteer fire companies, and is operated by the History Museum of Mobile. This restored 1855 firehouse is one of the few surviving examples of municipal architecture of the antebellum era. Visitors who then take a right on Canal Street, turn left (south) onto Broad Street, and travel for three miles will arrive at **Arlington Park** (Old Bayfront Drive) after passing through the old Brookley Air Force Base complex. This bayfront green space features a long boardwalk extending from the bluff and traversing the swampy shore of upper Mobile Bay just below the mouth of the Mobile River. This vantage point offers a magnificent view of Mobile Bay and its busy shipping channel, nearly the same view that enthralled visitors to Choctaw Point during the antebellum era. Choctaw Point, located less than two miles north of Arlington Park at the mouth of the Mobile River, is today occupied by a large loading facility for shipping containers. Obscuring much of the point is the adjoining McDuffie Island, created in the twentieth century by piling dredging spoils at Garrow's Bend. Modern industrial development and I-10 have obscured any remaining traces of the Old Shell Road that so many visitors took to reach this area before the Civil War.

Mobile has, of course, numerous other historic sites that will inform contemporary visitors who want to learn more about the city's past and better understand its heritage. These sites, though, help the modern visitor form an image of how the place may have appeared in the first half of the nineteenth century. They are some of the best places for gaining some notion of what visitors to the antebellum city may have seen in their travels.

Notes

Introduction

1. Thomason and McLaurin, *Mobile*, 55 (first quote), 41 (second quote); Delaney, *Remember Mobile*, 152 (third quote).
2. Amos, "Social Life," 55.
3. Bremer, *Homes of the New World,* 19 (first quote); Clinton, *Winter from Home*, 42 (second quote).

Chapter 1. Getting There

1. Summersell, *Mobile*, 16; Thomason and McLaurin, *Mobile*, 38; Gould, *From Fort to Port*, 28; Delaney, *Remember Mobile*, 151; Gosse, *Letters from Alabama*, 29 (quote). The first two steamboat production companies to operate in Mobile were the Mobile Steam-Boat Company and Navigation Steam-Boat Company.
2. Richards, *Appleton's Companion Hand-Book of Travel*, 128, 292; Nichols, *Forty Years of American Life*, 220, 229; Trautmann, "Alabama through a German's Eyes," 138; Lyell, *Second Visit to North America*, 52; Bernhard, *Travels through North America*, 31; Murray, *Letters from the United States*, 303; Martineau, *Society in America*, 66.
3. Lyell, *Second Visit to North America*, 45; Arfwedson, *United States and Canada*, 47.
4. Trautmann, "Alabama through a German's Eyes," 138; Lewis, *Impressions of America,* 162; Sledge, *Mobile River*, 103. Among the best sources on steamboats of the antebellum era are Adam I. Kane's *The Western River Steamboat* and Robert Gudmestad's Steamboats and the Rise of the Cotton Kingdom.
5. Shaw, *Ramble through the United States*, 211 (first quote); Lyell, *Second Visit to North America*, 47 (second quote); Nichols, *Forty Years of American Life*, 229 (third quote); Buckingham, *Slave States of America*, 263 (fourth quote).
6. Smith, *Theatrical Journey-Work and Anecdotical Recollections*, 136 (first quote); Fuller, *Belle Brittan on a Tour*, 114 (second quote).
7. Lyell, *Second Visit to North America*, 47; Fuller, *Belle Brittan on a Tour*, 114 (first quote); Thomas Hamilton, *Men and Manners in America*, 333; Nichols, *Forty Years of American Life*, 220; Featherstonhaugh, *Excursion through the Slave States*, 144 (second quote).
8. Stirling, *Letters from the Slave States*, 164 (first quote); Olmsted, *Journey*, 559 (second quote); Thomas Hamilton, *Men and Manners in America*, 331 (third quote); Featherstonhaugh, *Excursion through the Slave States*, 144 (fourth quote); Arfwedson, *United States and Canada*, 49–50 (fifth quote); Alexander Mackay, *Western World*, 267 (sixth quote); Wood, *Autobiography of William Wood*, 249 (seventh quote).

9. Viccars, "Swedish Writer Visits," 43 (first quote); Alexander Mackay, *Western World*, 269; (second quote).
10. Buckingham, *Slave States of America*, 264, 268; Lyell, *Second Visit to North America*, 48, 49 (second quote); Tasistro, *Random Shots and Southern Breezes*, 7 (first quote); Hall, *Travels in North America*, 309.
11. Lyell, *Second Visit to North America*, 49 (first quote); Power, *Impressions of America*, 156, 157 (second, third, and seventh quotes); Vassar, *Twenty Years around the World*, 220 (fourth and fifth quotes); Arfwedson, *United States and Canada*, 41; Alexander Mackay, *Western World*, 185; Basil Hall, *Travels in North America*, 310 (sixth quote).
12. Lewis, *Impressions of America*, 165, 167 (first quote); Robert Russell, *North America*, 282 (third quote); Lyell, *Second Visit to North America*, 51; Alexander Mackay, *Western World*, 189 (second quote).
13. Taylor, "Mobile," 129; Sledge, *Mobile River*, 108; Peter J. Hamilton, *Mobile of the Five Flags*, 269; Alexander Mackay, *Western World*, 189, (quote); Bernhard, *Travels through North America*, 31; Gaddis, *Foot-Prints of an Itinerant*, 337. The *Eliza Battle* is remembered today in part because of a famous Alabama ghost story, as told by the acclaimed folklorist Kathryn Tucker Windham in *Thirteen Alabama Ghosts and Jeffrey*. According to her now well-known tale, which was inspired by elements of other stories told about the boat for years, on certain dark nights the boat can still be seen silently drifting while aflame along remote stretches of the Tombigbee.
14. Fuller, *Belle Brittan on a Tour*, 111; Margaret Hall, *Aristocratic Journey*, 250 (first quote), 251 (second quote); Featherstonhaugh, *Excursion through the Slave States*, 142 (third quote); Macready, *Macready's Reminiscences*, 552–553 (fourth quote).
15. Robert Russell, *North America*, 282 (first quote); Shaw, *Ramble through the United States*, 214 (second and third quote); Murray, *Letters from the United States*, 303 (fourth quote); Kingsford, *Impressions of the West*, 66 (fifth quote).
16. Whipple, *Bishop Whipple's Southern Diary*, 83 (first quote); Ingraham, *Sunny South*, 541 (second quote); Pulszky and Pulszky, *White, Red, Black*, 114 (third quote); Alexander Mackay, *Western World*, 184 (fourth quote).
17. Nichols, *Forty Years of American Life*, 220 (first quote); Gosse, *Letters from Alabama*, 30 (second and fifth quotes); Thomas Hamilton, *Men and Manners in America*, 333 (third quote); Lewis, *Impressions of America*, 187 (fourth quote).

Chapter 2. Arrival

1. Lewis, *Impressions of America*, 166 (first quote); Everest, *Journey through the United States*, 113 (second quote); Ingraham, *Sunny South*, 504 (third quote); Gosse, *Letters from Alabama*, 24 (fourth quote); *The Traveller's Tour through the United States*, 33 (fifth quote); Buckingham, *America, Historical, Statistic, and Descriptive*, 274 (sixth quote).

2. Ingraham, *Sunny South*, 504 (first quote); Alexander Mackay, Western World, 280, (second quote); Bernhard, *Travels through North America*, 42 (third quote).
3. Sledge, *Mobile River*, 98–101; Thomason, *Mobile*, 70; Doss, *Cotton City*, 25; Olmsted, *Journey*, 567 (first quote); Vassar, *Twenty Years around the World*, 10 (second quote).
4. Oldmixon, *Transatlantic Wanderings*, 152 (first quote); Kellar, "Journey through theSouth," 363; Alexander Mackay, *Western World*, 284 (second quote); Ingraham, *Sunny South*, 502; Abbott, *South and North*, 91 (third quote).
5. Buckingham, *Slave States of America*, 292, 293 (first and second quotes); Ingraham, *Sunny South*, 502 (third quote); Abbott, *South and North*, 91 (fourth quote).
6. Nichols, *Forty Years of American Life*, 222 (first quote); Ker, *Travels through the Western Interior*, 334 (second quote); Arfwedson, *United States and Canada*, 46 (third quote); Thomason and McLaurin, *Mobile*, 38; Summersell, *Mobile*, 17; Sledge, *Mobile River*, 99; Delaney, *Remember Mobile*, 145.
7. Stuart, *Three Years in North America*, 111 (first quote); Bernhard, *Travels through North America*, 38; Murray, *Letters from the United States*, 302; Stuart, *Three Years in North America*, 117 (second quote).
8. Kingsford, *Impressions of the West*, 66; Murray, *Letters from the United States*, 303; Hodgson, *Letters from North America*, 152 (first quote); Bernhard, *Travels through North America*, 41 (second quote), 42 (third quote); Stuart, *Three Years in North America*, 122 (fourth quote).
9. Thomas Hamilton, *Men and Manners in America*, 328.
10. Lyell, *Second Visit to North America*, 45; Kellar, "Journey through the South," 363 (first quote), 364 (second quote); Power, *Impressions of America*, 161; Thomas Hamilton, *Men and Manners in America*, 328; Wortley, *Travels in the United States*, 134–135.
11. Kellar, "Journey through the South," 363.
12. Gould, *From Fort to Port*), 41, 42, 54, 72, 73, 113, 146–148; Thomasan, *Mobile*, 73; Doss, *Cotton City*, 44; Delaney, *Story of Mobile*, 85.
13. Thomason, *Mobile*, 73; Taylor, "Mobile," 42; Gould, *From Fort to Port*, 42.
14. Thomason, *Mobile*, 73; Gould, *From Fort to Port*, 148–149; Doss, *Cotton City*, 45; Delaney, *Remember Mobile*, 154; Amos, "Social Life," 166; Delaney, *Story of Mobile*, 86; Lanman, *Adventures in the Wilds*, 189. The original Battle House structure burned in 1905, and the contemporary hotel of the same name operates in the building that replaced it at the same location. In the mid-twentieth century, it underwent a thorough renovation after years of neglect and again stands as one of the region's most acclaimed hotels.
15. Murray, *Letters from the United States*, 303 (first quote); Power, *Impressions of America*, 211 (second quote); Ingraham, *Sunny South*, 504 (third quote); Olmsted, *Journey*, 566 (fourth quote); Fuller, *Belle Brittan on a Tour*, 114 (fifth quote).

16. Alexander Mackay, *Western World*, 281 (first quote); Power, *Impressions of America*, 224 (second quote); Buckingham, *Slave States of America*, 274 (third quote), 283 (fourth quote).
17. Wood, *Autobiography of William Wood*, 142 (first quote); Whipple, *Bishop Whipple's Southern Diary*, 91 (second and third quote); Margaret (Mrs. Basil) Hall, *Aristocratic Journey*, 245, 246 (fifth quote); Basil Hall, *Travels in North America*, 315 (fourth quote).
18. Welby, *Young Traveller's Journal*, 135 (second quote), 137 (first quote); Buckingham, *Slave States of America*, 283; Clinton, *Winter from Home*, 2, 42 (third quote).
19. Basil Hall, *Travels in North America*, 314 (first and second quotes); Pulszky and Pulszky, *White, Red, Black*, 110 (second quote).

Chapter 3. The Setting
1. Featherstonhaugh, *Excursion through the Slave States*, 143 (first and second quote); Welby, *Young Traveller's Journal*, 145 (third quote); Basil Hall, *Travels in North America*, 316 (fourth quote).
2. Bernhard, *Travels through North America*, 38 (first quote); Gosse, *Letters from Alabama*, 24 (second and third quotes); Lyell, *Second Visit to North America*, 108 (fourth quote). The Carolina parakeet, a small green neotropical species, could once be found throughout most of eastern North America. Populations of the bird appear to have already been in decline by the mid-nineteenth century in some locations. It was declared extinct in 1939. For more information about this bird, see Snyder, *Carolina Parakeet*.
3. Buckingham, *Slave States of America*, 273.
4. *National Gazette and Literary Register*, July 7, 1822, subject files, Jack Friend Research Library, History Museum of Mobile (first quote); Olliffe, *American Scenes*, 52 (second quote).
5. Shaw, *Ramble through the United States*, 215 (first and second quotes); Herz, *My Travels in America*, 97 (third quote).
6. Power, *Impressions of America*, 162 (first quote), 161 (second quote); Welby, *Young Traveller's Journal*, 144 (third quote); Charles Mackay, *Life and Liberty in America*, 181 (fourth quote).
7. Bremer, *Homes of the New World*, 18 (first and second quote), 19 (third quote); Oldmixon, *Transatlantic Wanderings*, 152 (fourth quote).
8. Shaw, *Ramble through the United States*, 214 (first, second, and third quotes); Bernhard, *Travels through North America*, 40 (fourth quote); *New York Spectator*, September 5, 1820; Lyell, *Second Visit to North America*, 102.
9. Ingraham, *Sunny South*, 505 (first quote); Buckingham, *Slave States of America*, 292 (second quote); Bremer, *Homes of the New World*, 17 (third quote), 20 (fourth quote).

10. Oldmixon, *Transatlantic Wanderings*, 156 (first quote), 158 (second quote); "A Trip to Mobile," *New Orleans Daily Picayune*, July 19, 1839, (third quote); "Letter from Mobile," *National Gazette and Literary Register*, July 7, 1822, (fourth quote).
11. "Madam LeVert's Diary," *Alabama Historical Quarterly* 3 (Spring 1941), 51–52 (quotes).
12. Margaret Hall, *Aristocratic Journey*, 246 (first quote); Robert Russell, *North America*, 283; *New York Times*, February 18, 1852 (second quote); Wood, *Autobiography of William Wood*, 142 (third quote).
13. Lyell, *A Second Visit to North America*, 106 (first quote); Olmsted, *Journey*, 566 (second quote); Nichols, *Forty Years of American Life*, 223 (third quote), 226 (sixth quote); Macready, *Macready's Reminiscences*, 553 (fourth quote); Murray, *Letters from the United States*, 303 (fifth quote).
14. Charles Mackay, *Life and Liberty in America*, 181 (first and last quote); Nichols, *Forty Years of American Life*, 223 (second quote), 226 (third quote); Ingraham, *Sunny South*, 511 (fourth quote); Vassar, *Twenty Years around the World*, 10 (fifth quote).
15. Sledge, *Mobile River*, 86; Doss, *Cotton City*, 99; Gould, *From Fort to Port*, 29, 43, 46; Gould, *From Builders to Architects*, 19–20; Sledge and Hagler, *Pillared City*, 25–26.
16. Doss, *Cotton City*, 16; Delaney, *Story of Mobile*, 68; Thomason, *Mobile*, 66; Erickson, *Mobile's Legal Legacy*, 32; Delaney, *Remember Mobile*, 139; Sledge, *Mobile River*, 90; Olmsted, *Journey*, 565 (quote).
17. Sledge, *Mobile River*, 90; Doss, *Cotton City*, 2; Thomason, *Mobile*, 78; Alexander Mackay, *Western World*, 280 (quote).
18. *Mobile Daily Register*, June 7, 1858 (first quote); Doss, *Cotton City*, 154; Gosse, *Letters from Alabama*, 26 (second quote); Oldmixon, *Transatlantic Wanderings*, 157 (third quote).
19. *Independent Chronicle and Boston Chronicle*, November 18, 1835; Gould, *From Fort to Port*, 57.
20. Sledge and Hagler, *Pillared City*, 27, 41; Gould, *From Fort to Port*, 38, , 138, 129 (quote).
21. Sledge and Hagler, *Pillared City*, 30, 48, 59; Gould, *From Fort to Port*, 75, 108; Doss, *Cotton City*, 164–166; Delaney, *Story of Mobile*, 80; Featherstonhaugh, *Excursion through the Slave States*, 143 (quote).
22. Power, *Impressions of America*, 164 (first and second quote); description of Mobile originally printed in the *Nashville Banner*, reprinted in the Mobile Commercial Register, February 19, 1828.
23. Delaney, *Story of Mobile*, 74; Doss, *Cotton City*, 139; Erickson, *Mobile's Legal Legacy*, 43; Delaney, *Remember Mobile*, 147; Power, *Impressions of America*, 223;

Alexander Mackay, *Western World*, 280 (first quote); Featherstonhaugh, *Excursion through the Slave States*, 143 (second and third quotes).
24. Taylor, "Mobile," 47; Gould, *From Fort to Port*, 31–32; Walton, "I Anticipate Nothing but Ruin," 44; Stirling, *Letters from the Slave States*, 178 (first quote); Whipple, *Bishop Whipple's Southern Diary*, 86 (second quote); Craighead, *Mobile*, 130.
25. Bernhard, *Travels through North America*, 39 (first quote), 41 (fourth quote); Whipple, *Bishop Whipple's Southern Diary*, 87 (second quote); Oldmixon, *Transatlantic Wanderings*, 154 (third quote); Doss, *Cotton City*, 43.
26. Amos, "Social Life," 29; Bremer, *Homes of the New World*, 20 (first quote); Featherstonhaugh, *Excursion through the Slave States*, 143 (second quote).
27. Murray, *Letters from the United States*, 303 (first quote); Buckingham, *Slave States of America*, 282 (second quote); Robert Russell, *North America*, 281 (third quote).
28. Featherstonhaugh, *Excursion through the Slave States*, 143 (first quote); Ingraham, *Sunny South*, 508 (second quote).
29. Gould, *From Fort to Port*, 49, 122; Gould, *From Builders to Architects*, 25; Thomason and McLaurin, *Mobile*, 42.
30. Oldmixon, *Transatlantic Wanderings*, 155 (first quote), 154 (second and third quotes); Abbott, *South and North*, 113 (fourth quote); Gosse, *Letters From Alabama*, 26 (fifth quote); Pulszky and Pulszky, *White, Red, Black*, 112 (sixth quote); Featherstonhaugh, *Excursion through the Slave States*, 143 (seventh quote); Nichols, *Forty Years of American Life*, 222 (eighth quote).
31. Gould, *From Fort to Port*, 31, 47; Ker, *Travels through the Western Interior*, 334; Alexander Mackay, *Western World*, 281; Bernhard, *Travels through North America*, 39 (first quote); Herz, *My Travels in America*, 97 (second quote).
32. Sherman, *Home Letters of General Sherman*, 23 (first quote); Wortley, *Travels in the United States*, 132; Olmsted, *Journey*, 565; Ingraham, *Sunny South*, 506; Lanman, *Adventures in the Wilds*, 189 (second quote).

Chapter 4. A Place for Business

1. Sledge and Hagler, *Pillared City*, 95 (first quote); Fuller, *Belle Brittan on a Tour*, 112 (second quote).
2. *National Intelligencer*, September 12, 1816 (first quote); Levasseur, *Lafayette in America*, 95 (second quote); Arfwedson, *United States and Canada*, 45 (third quote); Buckingham, *America, Historical, Statistic, and Descriptive*, 281 (fourth quote); *Niles Weekly Register* 12 (1817): 240 (fifth quote).
3. Ingraham, *Sunny South*, 507 (first quote); Mackay, *Western World*, 280 (second quote); Oldmixon, *Transatlantic Wanderings*, 156 (third quote); Wortley, *Travels in the United States*, 132 (fourth quote); Lanman, *Adventures in the Wilds*, 190 (fifth quote); Power, *Impressions of America*, 211 (sixth quote).

4. Parker, "Blakeley"; Hiatt, "Blakeley"; Bunn, *Historic Blakeley State Park*.
5. Hodgson, *Letters from North America*, 151 (first quote); Morse and Morse, *Traveller's Guide*, 36 (second and third quotes).
6. Morris, *Wanderings of a Vagabond*, 460 (first and second quote); Bernhard, *Travels through North America*, 39 (third quote); Olliffe, *American Scenes*, 52 (fourth quote).
7. Martineau, *Society in America*, 65; Amos, "Social Life," 30–35; Thomason, Mobile, 70–71, 75; Doss, *Cotton City*, 22.
8. Doss, *Cotton City*, 20–22; Gould, *From Fort to Port*, 27; Taylor, "Mobile," 140; Griffith, Alabama, 213; Amos, "Social Life," 60; Thomason, *Mobile*, 70, 73; Delaney, *Story of Mobile*, 64.
9. Griffith, *Alabama*, 214; Buckingham, *Slave States of America*, 283; Thomas Hamilton, *Men and Manners in America*, 328 (first quote); Charles Mackay, *Life and Liberty in America*, 180 (second quote); Gosse, *Letters from Alabama*, 26 (third quote); Sledge, *Mobile River*, 93 (fourth quote).
10. Doss, *Cotton City*, 22, 24, 30, 212; Thomason, *Mobile*, 75, 76, 89; Amos, "Social Life," 61; Summersell, *Mobile*, 15; Thomason and McLaurin, *Mobile*, 41.
11. Doss, *Cotton City*, 81; Olmsted, *Journey*, 566–567 (quotes).
12. Amos, "Social Life," 17; Gould, *From Fort to Port*, 27, 28, 39, 110, Doss, *Cotton City*, 15, 27; Thomason, *Mobile*, 69, 71; Sledge, *Mobile River*, 94; Summersell, *Mobile*, 22; Peter J. Hamilton, *Mobile of the Five Flags*, 270; Arfwedson, *United States and Canada*, 47; Bernhard, *Travels through North America*, 40.
13. Gould, *From Fort to Port*, 33; Thomason, *Mobile*, 69, 72; Doss, *Cotton City*, 28. 31–38; Taylor, "Mobile," 30.
14. Arfwedson, *United States and Canada*, 45 (first quote); Doss, *Cotton City*, 18; Kellar, "Journey through the South," 363 (second quote).
15. Charles Mackay, *Life and Liberty in America*, 180 (first and second quote); Sledge, *Mobile River*, 90; Oldmixon, *Transatlantic Wanderings*, 167 (third quote).
16. Abbott, *South and North*, 134 (first quote); Amos, "Social Life," 99; Taylor, "Mobile," 32; Sledge, *Mobile River*, 95; Ingraham, *Sunny South*, 504 (second quote).
17. Thomas Hamilton, *Men and Manners in America*, 329 (first quote); Amos, "Social Life," 59 (second quote); Charles Mackay, *Life and Liberty in America*, 180 (third and fourth quotes); Ingraham, *Sunny South*, 507 (fifth quote); Morse and Morse, *Traveller's Guide,* 202 (sixth quote).
18. Whipple, Bishop *Whipple's Southern Diary*, 86 (first quote); Thomas Hamilton, *Men and Manners in America*, 329 (second quote); Lanman, *Adventures in the Wilds*, 189 (third quote).
19. Gould, *From Fort to Port*, 32; Doss, *Cotton City*, 82, 213, 216; Amos, "Social Life," 93; Sledge, *Mobile River*, 91; Thomason, *Mobile*, 91.

20. Thomason, *Mobile*, 87; Doss, *Cotton City*, 195–196, 207; Thomason and McLaurin, *Mobile*, 54.
21. Amos, "Social Life," 51; Vassar, *Twenty Years around the World*, 10 (first quote); Power, *Impressions of America*, 224 (second quote); Bernhard, *Travels through North America*, 41 (third quote); Lanman, *Adventures in the Wilds*, 190 (fourth quote).

Chapter 5. Dangers

1. Lyell, *Second Visit to North America*, 103 (quote).
2. Arfwedson, *United States and Canada*, 46 (first quote); Ker, *Travels through the Western Interior*, 333 (second quote); Koch, *Journey through a Part*, 109 (third quote).
3. Stuart, *Three Years in North America*, 123 (quote). Several books examine specific yellow fever epidemics in American history, such as the deadly 1878 outbreak that devastated the city of Memphis and the Mississippi Valley. For an overview of the disease and its effects from the late 1700s to the twentieth century in the United States, see Pierce and Writer, *Yellow Jack*.
4. Smith, *Theatrical Management in the West*, 104 (first quote); Lyell, *Second Visit to North America*, 107 (second quote).
5. Doss, *Cotton City*, 156–157; Amos, "Social Life," 19, 38; Summersell, *Mobile*, 26; Gould, *From Fort to Port*, 117; Delaney, *Story of Mobile*, 76; Walton, "I Anticipate Nothing but Ruin," 61; Hodgson, *Letters from North America*, 155; Herz, *My Travels in America*, 96 (quote).
6. *New York Spectator*, September 5, 1820 (first quote); Lewis, *Impressions of America*, 172 (second quote); Lyell, *Second Visit to North America*, 107 (third quote); Abbott, *South and North*, 113 (fourth quote).
7. Everest, *Journey through the United States*, 113 (first quote); Robert Russell, *North America*, 281 (second quote).
8. Doss, *Cotton City*, 159, 160, 171, 173; Taylor, "Mobile," 5, 113, 115, 116, 125; Amos, "Social Life," 131; Thomason, *Mobile*, 84; Lewis, *Impressions of America*, 172; Alexander Mackay, *Western World*, 280 (quote).
9. *Mobile Commercial Register*, February 7, 1822 (first quote); Gould, *From Fort to Port*, 50; Featherstonhaugh, *Excursion through the Slave States*, 143 (second quote); Alexander Mackay, *Western World*, 281 (third quote). For a brief history of the Spring Hill neighborhood, see Barney, *The Hill*.
10. Gould, *From Fort to Port*, 35; Delaney, *Story of Mobile*, 76; *Richmond Enquirer*, September 26, 1820 (quotes). The article was a reprint of a story which originally appeared in a local paper.
11. Amos, "Social Life," 20, 39; Thomason, *Mobile*, 66; Gould, *From Fort to Port*, 103; Doss, *Cotton City*, 152; Peter J. Hamilton, *Mobile of the Five Flags*, 234; Erick-

son, *Mobile's Legal Legacy*, 41; *North American Tourist*, 458; Lewis, *Impressions of America*, 73; Ludlow, *Dramatic Life*, 511; Lyell, *Second Visit to North America*, 107 (quote).
12. Thomason, *Mobile*, 66–68; Doss, *Cotton City*, 16–17, 154; Gould, *From Fort to Port*, 34, 77; Summersell, *Mobile*, 26.
13. Hall, *Travels in North America*, 313 (first quote); Buckingham, *Slave States of America*, 287; Stuart, *Three Years in North America*, 123 (second quote); Thomas Hamilton, *Men and Manners in America*, 328 (third quote).
14. Oldmixon, *Transatlantic Wanderings*, 153 (first quote); Arfwedson, *United States and Canada*, 44 (second quote).
15. Buckingham, *Slave States of America*, 286; Cleveland, "Social Conditions in Alabama," 21–22; Taylor, "Mobile," 81, 90.
16. Power, *Impressions of America*, 219–220; *New Orleans Daily Picayune*, April 2, 1839; Buckingham, *Slave States of America*, 285 (quote).
17. Peter J. Hamilton, *Mobile of the Five Flags*, 276; Doss, *Cotton City*, 43, 140; Thomason, *Mobile*, 83; Morris, *Wanderings of a Vagabond*, 461–462 (quotes); Cleveland, "Social Conditions in Alabama," 21; Taylor, "Mobile," 79, 90; Doss, *Cotton City*, 140–143; Lewis, *Impressions of America*, 171.
18. Buckingham, *Slave States of America*, 287 (quote).

Chapter 6. People and Lifestyles
1. Lanman, *Adventures in the Wilds*, 189 (quotes).
2. Thomason and McLaurin, *Mobile*, 36; Thomason, *Mobile*, 65; Erickson, *Mobile's Legal Legacy*, 34; Gould, *From Fort to Port*, 30, 131; Summersell, *Mobile*, 12, 24, 39; Doss, *Cotton City*, 193; Taylor, "Mobile," 1, 104; Gould, *From Builders to Architects*, 25; *Manufacturers and Farmer's Journal and Providence and Nantucket Advertiser*, December 9, 1835 (quote).
3. Thomason, *Mobile*, 78–80; Doss, Cotton City, 89, 116; Delaney, *Remember Mobile*, 143.
4. Thomason and McLaurin, *Mobile*, 37; Sledge, *Mobile River*, 96.
5. Whipple, *Bishop Whipple's Southern Diary*, 84 (fifth quote), 86 (first quote); Shaw, *Ramble through the United States*, 215 (second quote); Morris, *Wanderings of a Vagabond*, 460 (third quote), 470 (fourth quote).
6. Thomason, *Mobile*, 76; Doss, *Cotton City*, 3, 54–55; Taylor, "Mobile," 150.
7. Amos, "Social Life," 44, 48; Summersell, *Mobile*, 39, 42; Thomason, *Mobile*, 78, 84; Doss, *Cotton City*, 64, 96, 105–106, 178; Oldmixon, *Transatlantic Wanderings*, 155.
8. Amos, "Social Life," 15 (first quote); Thomason, *Mobile*, 65; Gosse, *Letters from Alabama*, 25 (second quote); Doss, *Cotton City*, xv; Delaney, *Story of Mobile*, 74; Walton, "I Anticipate Nothing but Ruin," 45; Alexander Mackay, *Western World*, 281 (third quote); Ker, *Travels through the Western Interior*, 333 (fourth quote).

9. Abbott, *South and North*, 113 (first quote); Lanman, *Adventures in the Wilds*, 190 (second quote); Ingraham, *Sunny South*, 504 (third quote); Lewis, *Impressions of America*, 178; Thomas Hamilton, *Men and Manners in America*, 331 (fourth and fifth quotes); Olmsted, *Journey*, 567 (sixth quote); Charles Mackay, *Life and Liberty in America*, 181 (seventh quote).
10. Lanman, *Adventures in the Wilds*, 190 (quotes).
11. Delaney, *Story of Mobile*, 77; Amos, "Social Life," 23; Thomason and McLaurin, *Mobile*, 44; Welby, *Young Traveller's Journal*, 136; *New York Times*, February 18, 1852 (quotes).
12. Welby, *Young Traveller's Journal*, 137 (quotes).
13. Ibid., 138 (second quote), 140 (first quote), 153; Wortley, *Travels in the United States*, 133 (third quote).
14. Wortley, *Travels in the United States*, 133 (first quote); Welby, *Young Traveller's Journal*, 139 (second and third quote), 146 (fourth quote).
15. Thomas Hamilton, *Men and Manners in America*, 328 (first, second, and third quotes); Oldmixon, *Transatlantic Wanderings*, 157 (fourth quote).
16. Lanman, *Adventures in the Wilds*, 190 (quotes); Welby, *Young Traveller's Journal*, 145; Herz, My *Travels in America*, 97 (fourth quote).
17. Lanman, *Adventures in the Wilds*, 190 (first quote); Amos, "Social Life," 24, Delaney, *Story of Mobile*, 78; Charles Mackay, *Life and Liberty in America*, 185 (second quote); Bernhard, *Travels through North America*, 40 (third quote); Welby, *Young Traveller's Journal*, 136.
18. Whipple, *Bishop Whipple's Southern Diary*, 87–88 (first and second quotes); Hodgson, *Letters from North America*, 153 (third quote); Olmsted, *Journey*, 560 (fourth and fifth quotes); Everest, *Journey through the United States*, 113 (sixth quote).
19. Ingraham, *Sunny South*, 500 (first quote), 506–507 (second, third, and fourth quotes), 512 (seventh quote); Buckingham, *Slave States of America*, 284 (fifth quote); Abbott, *South and North*, 114 (sixth quote); Oldmixon, *Transatlantic Wanderings*, 158 (eighth quote).
20. Buckingham, *Slave States of America*, 284 (first quote); Alexander Mackay, *Western World*, 281 (second quote); *New York Spectator*, September 5, 1820 (third and fourth quotes); Whipple, *Bishop Whipple's Southern Diary*, 90 (fifth quote); Hodgson, *Letters from North America*, 152 (sixth quote); Abbott, *South and North*, 114 (seventh quote).
21. "Letter from Mobile," *National Gazette and Literary Register*, July 7, 1822; Stuart, *Three Years in North America*, 124; Buckingham, *Slave States of America*, 225 (first quote); Margaret Hall, *Aristocratic Journey*, 248 (second quote); Hodgson, *Letters from North America*, 153; Kingsford, *Impressions of the West*, 66.

22. Taylor, "Mobile," 15, 22, 156; Thomason, *Mobile*, 68, 81; Doss, *Cotton City*, 63–64, 104, 176–177; Delaney, *Story of Mobile*, 84.
23. Nichols, *Forty Years of American Life*, 223; Hodgson, *Letters from North America*, 149 (first quote); Hodgson, *Remarks during a Journey*, 59 (second quote); Thomason, *Mobile*, 68; Thomason and McLaurin, *Mobile*, 38, 49–50; Gould, *From Fort to Port*, 44; Doss, *Cotton City*, 67, 111; Korn, *Jews of Mobile*, 20, 39, 54.
24. Bernhard, *Travels through North America*, 40 (first quote); Gould, *From Fort to Port*, 45, 68–69, 113; Buckingham, *Slave States of America*, 283 (second quote); Wood, *Autobiography of William Wood*, 142 (third quote).
25. Morris, *Wanderings of a Vagabond*, 460 (first quote); Power, *Impressions of America*, 225 (second quote); Lewis, *Impressions of America*, 184 (third, fourth, and fifth quotes), 167 (sixth and seventh quotes).
26. Whipple, *Bishop Whipple's Southern Diary*, 91 (first quote); Lewis, *Impressions of America*, 166 (second quote); Robert Russell, *North America*, 281 (third quote).
27. Buckingham, *Slave States of America*, 282 (quote), 289, Hodgson, *Letters from North America*, 393; Hodgson, *Remarks during a Journey*, 59; Thomason, *Mobile*, 85; Gould, *From Fort to Port*, 10, 63, 66, 101, 131; Doss, *Cotton City*, 218; Summersell, *Mobile*, 31; Gaillard, Gaillard, and Gaillard, *Mobile and the Eastern Shore*, 13. The Medical College of Alabama later moved to Birmingham and is now known as the University of Alabama at Birmingham School of Medicine.
28. Summersell, *Mobile*, 38–39.
29. Kingsford, *Impressions of the West*, 67 (first quote); Bernhard, *Travels through North America*, 39 (second quote); Featherstonhaugh, *Excursion through the Slave States*, 143 (third quote); Sherman, *Home Letters of General Sherman*, 21 (fourth quote).
30. Buckingham, *Slave States of America*, 290 (second quote), 451 (first quote).

Chapter 7. Slavery and the Enslaved

1. Delaney, *Story of Mobile*, 94; Doss, *Cotton City*, 86–87; Thomason, *Mobile*, 80; Amos, "Social Life," 43.
2. Nichols, *Forty Years of American Life*, 221; Murray, *Letters from the United States*, 304 (quotes).
3. Murray, *Letters from the United States*, 304 (quotes), 306.
4. Vassar, *Twenty Years around the World*, 10 (first quote); Robert Russell, *North America*, 281 (second quote); Kellar, "Journey through the South," 363 (third quote).
5. Bremer, *Homes of the New World*, 20 (first quote); Wortley, *Travels in the United States*, 136 (second quote); Welby, *Young Traveller's Journal*, 136.
6. Sellers, *Slavery in Alabama*, 199, 296; Thomason, *Mobile*, 78–80; Doss, *Cotton City*, 88–89, 92, 97, 146.

150 Notes to Chapters Seven and Eight

7. Nichols, *Forty Years of American Life*, 227 (first quote); Abbott, *South and North*, 112 (second quote).
8. Abbott, *South and North*, 93 (first and second quotes), 94 (third quote); Lyell, *Second Visit to North America*, 67 (fourth quote).
9. Hodgson, *Letters from North America*, 153 (first and second quotes); Bernhard, *Travels through North America*, 39 (third quote); Thomas Hamilton, *Men and Manners in America*, 331 (fourth quote); Lewis, *Impressions of America*, 174.
10. Taylor, "Mobile," 55; American Anti-Slavery Society, *American Slavery as It Is*, 62, 73.
11. Olmsted, *Journey*, 570; Everest, *Journey through the United States*, 113 (quote).
12. Thomason, *Mobile*, 79; Doss, *Cotton City*, 85; Sellers, *Slavery in Alabama*, 154; Bremer, *Homes of the New World*, 21 (quote).
13. Charles Howland Russell, *Memoir of Charles H. Russell*, 71 (quotes).
14. Whipple, *Bishop Whipple's Southern Diary*, 88–90 (quotes).
15. Stirling, *Letters from the Slave States*, 178 (first quote); Pulszky and Pulszky, *White, Red, Black*, 111–112 (remaining quotes).
16. Pulszky and Pulszky, *White, Red, Black*, 112 (first quote); Lewis, *Impressions of America*, 185 (second quote); Nichols, *Forty Years of American Life*, 222 (third quote).
17. Buckingham, *Slave States of America*, 264 (quotes); Thomason, *Mobile*, 98; Doss, *Cotton City*, 62.
18. Morris, *Wanderings of a Vagabond*, 467–468 (quotes), 470.
19. Ibid., 472–491, 489 (first quote), 491 (second quote).
20. Hodgson, *Letters from North America*, 155 (quotes).
21. Doss, *Cotton City*, 90; Thomason, *Mobile*, 80; Gould, *From Builders to Architects*, 25. The Adams-Onis Treaty officially ceded all Spanish possessions east of the Mississippi to the United States, including those already taken by force and appended to U.S. territories and states, and defined the new boundary between the United States and New Spain along the Gulf at the Sabine River. Among its several provisions, it guaranteed the rights of all residents of former Spanish territory officially conveyed to the United States.
22. Doss, *Cotton City*, 97, 147, 185, 189; Delaney, *Remember Mobile*, 140.
23. Buckingham, *Slave States of America*, 479–480 (quote).

Chapter 8. Entertainment and Celebrations

1. Sledge, *Mobile River*, 97.
2. Charles Mackay, *Life and Liberty in America*, 181 (first quote); Wood, *Autobiography of William Wood*, 143 (second quote); Welby, *Young Traveller's Journal*, 143 (third quote); Wortley, *Travels in the United States*, 133 (fourth quote); Pulszky and Pulszky, *White, Red, Black*, 112 (fifth quote).

3. Oldmixon, *Transatlantic Wanderings*, 155 (first quote); Margaret Hall, *Aristocratic Journey*, 247 (second quote); Vassar, *Twenty Years around the World*, 10 (third quote); Fuller, *Belle Brittan on a Tour*, 114.
4. Thomason, *Mobile*, 73; Taylor, "Mobile," 9, 10; Thomason and McLaurin, *Mobile*, 38, 45; Doss, *Cotton City*, 47; Gould, *From Fort to Port*, 39–40; Ludlow, *Dramatic Life*, 364, 492; Morris, *Wanderings of a Vagabond*, 460.
5. Ludlow, *Dramatic Life*, 268, 287, 427, 434; Thomason, *Mobile*, 70; Sledge, *Mobile River*, 97; Smith, *Theatrical Journey-Work and Anecdotical Recollections*, 76.
6. Bremer, *Homes of the New World*, 19–21 (first quote); Whipple, *Bishop Whipple's Southern Diary*, 87 (second quote); Smith, *Theatrical Journey-Work and Anecdotal Recollections*, 75 (third quote); Morris, *Wanderings of a Vagabond*, 15 (fourth quote).
7. Thomason, *Mobile*, 75; Amos, "Social Life," 170; Bremer, *Homes of the New World*, 20 (first quote); Nichols, *Forty Years of American Life*, 225 (second quote); Fuller, *Belle Brittan on a Tour*, 112 (third quote); Wortley, *Travels in the United States*, 135 (fourth quote). The best source of information on the life of LeVert is Paula Webb's *Such a Woman*.
8. Fuller, *Belle Brittan on a Tour*, 113 (first quote); Pulszky and Pulszky, *White, Red, and Black*, 111 (second quote); Bremer, *Homes of the New World*, 22–23 (third and fourth quotes).
9. A. J. Wright, "Gardner Quincy Colton's 1848 Visit to Mobile," Jack Friend Research Library, History Museum of Mobile subject files; Taylor, "Mobile," 12–13; Bernhard, *Travels through North America*, 40 (quote).
10. Sledge and Hagler, *Pillared City*, 41; Taylor, "Mobile," 14–15; Thomason and McLaurin, *Mobile*, 45.
11. Morris, *Wanderings of a Vagabond*, 460 (last quote), 462 (first quote); Buckingham, *Slave States of America*, 287 (second quote); Robert Russell, *North America*, 281 (third quote).
12. Doss, *Cotton City*, 150; Morris, *Wanderings of a Vagabond*, 459, 462 (quotes).
13. Taylor, "Mobile," 82; Thomason and McLaurin, *Mobile*, 47; Doss, *Cotton City*, 148; Morris, *Wanderings of a Vagabond*, 229 (first quote), 230 (third quote), 459 (second quote), 461 (sixth quote); Sledge, *Mobile River*, 98; Whipple, *Bishop Whipple's Southern Diary*, 84 (fifth quote), 87 (fourth quote).
14. Doss, *Cotton City*, 149; Morris, *Wanderings of a Vagabond*, 461 (quote).
15. Higginbotham, *Mobile, City by the Bay*, 52; Thomason and McLaurin, *Mobile*, 39; Ludlow, *Dramatic Life*, 263 (quote).
16. Levasseur, *Lafayette in America*, 95 (quotes), 97–98; Higginbotham, *Mobile, City by the Bay*, 53–54; Ludlow, *Dramatic Life*, 263; Delaney, *Remember Mobile*, 144.
17. Presidential Visits to Mobile subject files, Minnie Mitchell Library, Historic Mobile Preservation Society.

18. Polk, *Diary of James K. Polk*, 398–399.
19. Ludlow, *Dramatic Life*, 263 (first quote); Power, *Impressions of America*, 224; Bernhard, *Travels through North America*, 41; Taylor, "Mobile," 19; Whipple, *Bishop Whipple's Southern Diary*, 90 (second quote); Buckingham, *Slave States of America*, 290 (third quote).
20. Thomason and McLaurin, *Mobile*, 46; Thomason, *Mobile*, 74–75; Delaney, *Remember Mobile*, 157; Delaney, *Story of Mobile*, 74. For an introduction to Mobile's rich Mardi Gras history, see Roberts, *Mardi Gras in Mobile*.
21. Welby, *Young Traveller's Journal*, 137 (first and second quotes); Wortley, *Travels in the United States*, 132–133 (third and fourth quotes); *New York Daily Times*, January 14, 1852.

Bibliography

Abbott, John S. C. *South and North; Or, Impressions Received during a Trip to Cuba and the South*. New York: Abbey and Abbott, 1860.

Acker, Marian Francis. *Etchings of Old Mobile*. Mobile: Gill Printing, 1938.

American Anti-Slavery Society. *American Slavery as It Is: Testimony of a Thousand Witnesses*. New York: American Anti-Slavery Society, 1839.

Amos, Harriet E. "Social life in an Antebellum Cotton Port: Mobile, Alabama, 1820–1860." PhD diss., Emory University, 1976.

Arfwedson, Carl David. *The United States and Canada, in 1832, 1833, and 1834*. London: Richard Bentley, 1834.

Barney, William Howard. *The Hill: A History of Mobile's Exclusive Suburb*. N.p.: Office Supplies, 1999.

Bernhard, Duke of Saxe-Weimar Eisenach. *Travels through North America during the Years 1825 and 1826*. Philadelphia: Carey, Lea and Carey, 1828.

Bremer, Fredrika. *Homes of the New World*. London: Arthur Hall, Virtue, 1853.

Buckingham, James Silk. *America, Historical, Statistic, and Descriptive*. London: Fisher, Son, 1841.

———. *The Slave States of America*. London: Fisher, Son, 1842.

Bunn, Mike. *Historic Blakeley State Park: A Guide to the History and Heritage*. Spanish Fort, Ala.: Historic Blakeley State Park, 2017.

Cleveland, Gordon Baylor. "Social Conditions in Alabama as Seen by Travelers, 1840–1850." *Alabama Review* 2 no. 1 (January 1949): 3–23.

Clinton, Charles A. *A Winter from Home*. New York: John F. Trow, 1852.

Craighead, Erwin. *Mobile: Fact and Fiction*. Mobile: Powers Printing, 1930.

Delaney, Caldwell. *Remember Mobile*. Illustrated by Clark S. Whistler. Mobile: Haunted Book Shop, 1980. First published in 1948.

———. *The Story of Mobile*. Mobile: Haunted Book Shop, 1981.

Doss, Harriet E. Amos. *Cotton City: Urban Development in Antebellum Mobile*. Tuscaloosa: University of Alabama Press, 2001. First published in 1985.

Erickson, Ben. *Mobile's Legal Legacy: Three Hundred Years of Law in the Port City*. Birmingham, Ala.: Association Publishing, 2008.

Everest, Robert. *A Journey through the United States and Part of Canada*. London: John Chapman, 1855.

Featherstonhaugh, G. W. *Excursion through the Slave States, From Washington on the Potomac to the Frontier of Mexico; With Sketches of Popular Manners and Geological Notices*. New York: Harper and Brothers, 1844.

Fuller, Hiram. *Belle Brittan on a Tour at Newport, and Here and There*. New York: Derby and Jackson, 1858.

Gaddis, Maxwell Pierson. *Foot-Prints of an Itinerant*. Cincinnati, Ohio: Methodist Book Concern, 1855.

Gaillard, Frye, Nancy Gaillard, and Tracy Gaillard. *Mobile and the Eastern Shore*. Charleston, S.C.: Arcadia Press, 2003.

Gosse, Philip Henry. *Letters from Alabama, Chiefly Relating to Natural History*. London: Morgan and Chase, 1859.

Gould, Elizabeth Barrett. *From Builders to Architects: The Hobart-Hutchisson Six*. Montgomery, Ala.: Black Belt Press, 1997.

———. *From Fort to Port: An Architectural History of Mobile, Alabama, 1711–1918*. Tuscaloosa: University of Alabama Press, 1988.

Griffith, Lucille. *Alabama: A Documentary History to 1900*. Tuscaloosa: University of Alabama Press, 1972.

Gudmestad, Robert. *Steamboats and the Rise of the Cotton Kingdom*. Baton Rouge: Louisiana State University Press, 2011.

Gums, Bonnie L., Gregory A. Waselkov, and Sarah B. Mattics. *Planning for the Past: An Archaeological Resource Management Plan for the City of Mobile, Alabama*. Mobile: University of South Alabama, 1999.

Hall, Basil. *Travels in North America, in the Years 1827 and 1828*. Edinburgh: Cadell, 1829.

Hall, Margaret (Mrs. Basil). *The Aristocratic Journey: Being the Outspoken Letters of Mrs. Basil Hall Written during a Fourteen Months' Sojourn in America, 1827–1828*. Edited by Una Pope-Hennessy. New York: G. P. Putnam's Sons, 1931.

Hamilton, Peter J. *Mobile of the Five Flags; the Story of the River Basin and Coast about Mobile from the Earliest Times to the Present*. Mobile: Gill Printing, 1913.

Hamilton, Thomas. *Men and Manners in America*. Philadelphia: Carey, Lea and Blanchard, 1833.

Herz, Henri. *My Travels in America*. Translated by Henry Bertram Hill. Madison: State Historical Society of Wisconsin, 1963.

Hiatt, Grant D. "Blakeley." *Encyclopedia of Alabama*. February 24, 2011. http://encyclopedia ofalabama.org/article/h-3023.

Higginbotham, Jay. *Mobile, City by the Bay*. Mobile: Azalea City Printers, 1968.

Hodgson, Adam. *Letters from North America, Written during a Tour in the United States and Canada*. London: Hurst, Robinson, 1824.

———. *Remarks during a Journey through North America in the Years 1819, 1820, and 1821, in a Series of Letters*. New York: Samuel Whiting, 1823.

Hone, Philip. *The Diary of Philip Hone, 1828–1851*. Edited by Bayard Tuckerman. New York: Dodd, Mead, 1889.

Ingraham, J. H. *The Sunny South; Or, the Southerner at Home, Embracing Five Years' Experience of a Northern Governess in the Land of the Sugar and the Cotton*. Philadelphia: G. G. Evans, 1860.

Kane, Adam I. *The Western River Steamboat*. College Station: Texas A&M University Press, 2004.

Kellar, Herbert A. "A Journey through the South in 1836: Diary of James D. Davidson." *Journal of Southern History* 1, no. 3 (1935): 345–77.

Ker, Henry. *Travels through the Western Interior of the United States, From the Year 1803 up to the Year 1816, with a Particular Description of a Great Part of Mexico, or New Spain*. Elizabethtown, N.J.: Henry Ker, 1816.

Kingsford, William. *Impressions of the West and South, During a Six Weeks' Holiday*. Toronto: A. H. Armour, 1858.

Koch, Albert C. *Journey through a Part of the United States of North America in the Years 1844 to 1846*. Carbondale: Southern Illinois University Press, 1972.

Korn, Bertram Wallace. *The Jews of Mobile, 1763–1841*. New York: Hebrew Union College Press, 1970.

Lanman, Charles. *Adventures in the Wilds of the United States and British American Provinces*. Philadelphia: John W. Moore, 1856.

Levasseur, A. *Lafayette in America, in 1824 and 1825*. New York: White, Gallaher and White, 1829.

Lewis, George. *Impressions of America and the American Churches*. Edinburgh: W. P. Kennedy, 1845.

Ludlow, Noah M. *Dramatic Life as I Found It*. St. Louis, Mo.: G. I. Jones, 1880.

Lyell, Charles. *A Second Visit to North America*. London: John Murray, 1855.

Mackay, Alexander. *The Western World, Or, Travels in the United States in 1846–47: Exhibiting Them in Their Latest Development, Social, Political, and Industrial*. London: Richard Bentley, 1849.

Mackay, Charles. *Life and Liberty in America: Sketches on a Tour in the United States and Canada in 1857–1858*. New York: Harper and Brothers, 1859.

Macready, William Charles. *Macready's Reminiscences, and Selections from His Diaries and Letters*. Edited by Frederick Pollack. London: Macmillan, 1876.

"Madam LeVert's Diary." *Alabama Historical Quarterly* 3 (Spring 1941): 31–54.

Martineau, Harriet. *Society in America*. New York: Saunders and Otley, 1837.

McLaurin, Melton Alonza. *Mobile, the Life and Times of a Great Southern City: An Illustrated History*. Woodland Hills, Calif.: Windsor Publications, 1981.

Montule, Edward. *A Voyage to North America, and the West Indies, in 1817*. London: Sir Richard Phillips, 1821.

Morris, John. *Wanderings of a Vagabond: An Autobiography*. New York: John Morris, 1873.

Morse, Jedidiah, and Richard C. Morse. *The Traveller's Guide: Or Pocket Gazetter of the United States*. New Haven, Conn.: Nathan Whiting, 1823.

Murray, Amelia M. *Letters from the United States, Cuba and Canada*. New York: G. P. Putnam, 1856.

Nelson, Lucy G. *The History of Oakleigh, an Ante-bellum Mansion in Mobile*. Mobile: Gill Printing, 1956.

Nichols, Thomas L. *Forty Years of American Life*. London: John Maxwell, 1864.

Nolan, Charles E. *A History of the Archdiocese of Mobile*. Strasbourg, France: Éditions du Signe, 2012.

The North American Tourist. New York: A. T. Goodrich, 1839.

Oldmixon, John. *Transatlantic Wanderings: Or, A Last Look at the United States*. London: George Routledge, 1855.

Olliffe, Charles. *American Scenes: Eighteen Months in the New World*. Translation by Ernest Falbo and Lawrence A. Wilson. Painesville, Ohio: Lake Erie College Press, 1964. First published in 1853.

Olmsted, Frederick Law. *A Journey in the Seaboard Slave States, with Remarks on Their Economy*. New York: Dix and Edwards, 1856.

Parker, James C. "Blakeley: A Frontier Seaport." *Alabama Review*, January 27, 1974, 39–51.

Pierce, John R., and James V. Writer. *Yellow Jack: How Yellow Fever Ravaged America and Walter Reed Discovered Its Deadly Secrets*. Hoboken, N.J.: John Wiley and Sons, 2005.

Polk, James K. *The Diary of James K. Polk during His Presidency, 1845–1849*. Edited by Milo Milton Quaife. Chicago: A. C. McClurg, 1910.

Posey, Walter Brownlow, ed. *Alabama in the 1830s, as Recorded by British Travellers*. Birmingham, Ala.: Birmingham-Southern College, 1938.

Power, Tyrone. *Impressions of America, during the Years 1833, 1834, and 1835*. London: Richard Bentley, 1836.

Pulszky, Francis, and Theresa Pulszky. *White, Red, Black: Sketches of American Society in the United States during the Visit of Their Guests*. New York: Redfield, 1853.

Richards, T. Addison, ed. *Appleton's Companion Hand-Book of Travel: Containing a Full Description of the Principal Cities, Towns, and Places of Interest Together with Hotels and Routes of Travel through the United States and the Canadas*. New York: D. Appleton, 1864.

Roberts, L. Craig. *Mardi Gras in Mobile*. Mount Pleasant, S.C.: History Press, 2015.

Roche, Emma Langdon. *Historic Sketches of the South*. New York: Knickerbocker Press, 1914.

Russell, Charles Howland. *Memoir of Charles H. Russell*. New York: n.p., 1903.

Russell, Robert. *North America: Its Agriculture and Climate, Containing Observations on the Agriculture and Climate of Canada, the United States, and the Island of Cuba*. Edinburgh: Adam and Charles Black, 1857.

Sellers, James Benson. *Slavery in Alabama*. Tuscaloosa: University of Alabama Press, 1994.

Shaw, John. *A Ramble through the United States, Canada, and the West Indies*. London: Hope, 1856.

Sherman, William T. *Home Letters of General Sherman*. Edited by M. A. De Wolfe Howe. New York: Charles Scribner's Sons, 1909.

Sledge, John S. *The Mobile River*. Columbia: University of South Carolina Press, 2015.

Sledge, John S., and Sheila Hagler. *The Pillared City: Greek Revival Mobile*. Athens: University of Georgia Press, 2009.

Smith, Sol. *The Theatrical Journey-Work and Anecdotical Recollections of Sol Smith*. Philadelphia: T. B. Peterson, 1854.

———. *Theatrical Management in the West and South for Thirty Years*. New York: Harper and Brothers, 1868.

Snyder, Noel. *The Carolina Parakeet: Glimpses of a Vanished Bird*. Princeton, N.J.: Princeton University Press, 2004.

Stirling, James. *Letters from the Slave States*. London: John W. Parker and Son, 1857.

Stuart, James. *Three Years in North America*. New York: J. and J. Harper, 1833.

Summersell, C. G. *Mobile: History of a Seaport Town*. Tuscaloosa: University of Alabama Press, 1981.

Tasistro, Louis Fitzgerald. *Random Shots and Southern Breezes, Containing Critical Remarks on the Southern States and Southern Institutions, with Semi-Serious Observations of Men and Manners*. New York: Harper and Brothers, 1842.

Taylor, Paul Wayne. "Mobile: 1818-1859 as Her Newspapers Pictured Her." Master's thesis, University of Alabama, 1951.

Thomason, Michael V.R. *Historic Mobile: An Illustrated History of the Mobile Bay Region*. Toledo: Historical Publishing Network, 2010.

———. *Mobile: The New History of Alabama's First City*. Tuscaloosa: University of Alabama Press, 2001.

Thomason, Michael, and Alonza Melton McLaurin. *Mobile: American River City*. Mobile: Easter Publishing, 1975.

Thomason, Michael V.R., ed. *Down the Years: Articles on Mobile's History*. Mobile: Gulf Coast Historical Review, 2001.

Trautmann, Frederic. "Alabama through a German's Eyes: The Travels of Clara Von Gerstner, 1839." *Alabama Review* 36 (April 1983): 129–155.

The Traveller's Tour through the United States. New York: Roe Lockwood, 1842.

Vassar, John Guy. *Twenty Years around the World*. New York: Carleton, 1862.

Viccars, Marion. "A Swedish Writer Visits the Deep South." *Alabama Historical Quarterly* 38 (Spring 1976): 30–44.

Walton, Donnelly Lancaster. "'I Anticipate Nothing but Ruin and Destruction': Agricola Wilkins in 1830s Mobile." *Alabama Review* 73 no. 1 (2020): 40–68.

Webb, Paula Lenor. *Such a Woman: The Life of Madame Octavia Walton LeVert*. Mobile: Intellect Publishing, 2021.

Welby, Lady Victoria. *A Young Traveller's Journal of a Tour in North and South America during the Year 1850*. London: T. Bosworth, 1852.

Whipple, Henry Benjamin. *Bishop Whipple's Southern Diary, 1843–1844*. Edited by Lester B. Shippee. New York: Da Capo Press, 1968.

Williams, William. *Appleton's New and Complete United States Guidebook for Travellers*. New York: D. Appleton, 1850.

Windham, Kathryn Tucker. *Thirteen Alabama Ghosts and Jeffrey*. Tuscaloosa: University of Alabama Press, 1987.

Wood, William. *Autobiography of William Wood*. New York: J. S. Babcock, 1895.

Wortley, Lady Emmeline Stuart. *Travels in the United States, Etc. during 1849 and 1850*. New York: Harper and Brothers, 1868.

Zietz, Robert. *The Gates of Heaven: Congregation Sha'arai Shomayim, the first 150 years, Mobile, Alabama, 1844–1994*. Mobile: Congregation Sha'arai Shomayim, 1994.

Index

Abbott, John S. C., 24, 85, 104
African Methodist Church, 96
Alabama River, 8, 13, 19, 58, 66, 131
Alhambra Hotel, 123
American Hotel, 27
Arfwedson, C. D., 9
Arlington Park, 137
Auxiliary Tract Society, 91

Barton Academy, 97, 135
Bascombe Race Course, 123
Battle, James, 29
Battle, John, 29
Battle House Hotel, 29–30, 84, 132
Baymen's Society, 91
Ben Franklin (boat), 16
Ben May Public Library, 135
Bernhard, Duke Karl, 49, 53, 59, 97, 106
Betsy (enslaved woman), 103
Bienville, Jean-Baptiste Le Moyne, Sieur de, 133
Bienville Square, 133
Bishop Portier House, 134
Blakeley, Ala., 25–26, 57–58
Blakeley, Josiah, 57–58
Bragg, John, 136
Bragg-Mitchell Mansion, 136
Bremer, Fredrika, 5, 38–39, 40, 103, 108, 121, 123
Buckingham, James S., 32–33, 51, 76, 80, 96, 113, 128

Calhoun, John C., 126
Can't Get Away Club, 73
Cathedral Basilica of the Immaculate Conception, 95, 134
Cathedral Square, 134
Choctaw Indians, 86–89

Choctaw Point, 47, 118, 137
Christ Church, 95, 132
Church Street Graveyard, 135
Clay, Henry, 126
Clinton, Charles A., 5
Colton, Gardner Quincy, 123
Conde-Charlotte House, 132
Cooper Riverside Park, 131
Cowbellion de Rakin Society, 129, 130
Cox-Deasy Cottage, 135

Daughters of the American Revolution, 132
Daughters of the Stars, The (play), 121
Dauphin Island, 17
Davidson, James, 26, 27, 64, 102
Delaney, Caldwell, 3, 5
De Tonti Square Historic District, 132
Dog River Bar, 23
Doss, Harriet Amos, 5

Eliza Battle (boat), 16–17
Emeline (boat), 26
Emmanuel Street Synagogue, 94

Featherstonhaugh, George, 17, 35, 47, 49, 53, 97
Female Benevolent Society, 91
Fillmore, Millard, 126
fires, 46
Forrest, Mr., 114–115
Fort Conde, 45, 132
Fort Morgan, 97
Franklin Hall, 123
Franklin House Hotel, 27
Franklin Society, 91
Fuller, Hiram, 11, 30, 55

Garrow's Bend, 137

Globe Hotel, 27, 28
Gosse, Phillip Henry, 20, 36, 61, 84
Gould, Elizabeth Barrett, 5, 46
Government Street Presbyterian Church, 95, 96, 135
Gulf of Mexico, 9, 17
Gulfquest Maritime Museum, 131

Hall, Basil, 13, 32–33, 76
Hall, Margaret, 32–33, 42
Hamilton, Thomas, 20, 26, 61, 76–77, 85, 88, 106
Herz, Henri, 38, 54, 89
Hibernian Benevolent Society, 84, 91
Higginbotham, Jay, 5
Historic Mobile Preservation Society, 135
Historic Oakleigh Complex, 135
History Museum of Mobile, 132, 137
Hodgson, Adam, 25, 89, 90, 93, 96, 106, 115
Horta, Peter, 135

Indescribables, 129
Ingraham, Joseph Holt, 19, 30, 51, 54, 66, 85, 90

Jenny Lind in Heidelberg (play), 121
Jones, Israel, 95

Kent, George, 114–115
King, Rufus, 25
Kingsford, William, 97
Kraft, Michael, 129

Ladies Bethel Society, 91
Lafayette, Marquis de, 125
Lafayette Hotel, 27
Lake Borgne, 9
Lanman, Charles, 81, 85, 86, 88, 89
Le Clede Hotel, 27
Le Havre, France, 61

LeVert, Henry, 121
LeVert, Octavia, 41, 87, 97, 103, 121–123
Lewis, Addin, 84
Lewis, George, 95–96, 106
lighters, 23–24
Liverpool, England, 61
London, England, 61
Lower Fleet, 23
Ludlow, Noah, 119, 128
Ludlow's Theater, 116
Lyell, Charles, 9, 36, 40, 70

Mackay, Alexander, 85, 90
Mackay, Charles, 61, 64, 86, 89
Magnolia Cemetery, 136
Mansion House Hotel, 32
Mardi Gras, 91, 118, 128, 130
Mardi Gras Park, 132
Martineau, Harriet, 59
McDuffie Island, 137
Medical College of Alabama, 97
Meek, Alexander B., 97
Minnie Mitchell Archives, 135
Mississippi River, 9
Mississippi Territory, 3
Mobile: architecture in, 44–47, 50–54; charitable organizations in, 93; churches in, 93–96; cotton trade in, 55–66; fires in, 74–78; foreign population in, 84–86; free blacks in, 115–117; gambling in, 124–125; gardens in, 42; health conditions in, 69–74; holiday celebrations in, 128; hotels in, 27, 28–29, 30, 32–33; lawlessness in, 78–80; natural setting of, 118; population of, 81–82; racial diversity in, 86; railroads in, 67; recreation in, 118, 119–130; seasonal nature of population, 81–83; slave market in, 108–110, 132; slavery in, 99–115; society in, 81–97; streets in,

47–50; theaters in, 119–121; trees in, 43; waterfront, 13–14
Mobile Bay, 8, 9, 42, 58, 118, 119, 131, 137
Mobile Hotel, 27
Mobile Jockey Club, 124
Mobile Local History and Genealogy Library, 135
Mobile Medical Museum, 136
Mobile Mercantile Advertiser, 98
Mobile River, 19, 26, 137; dredging in, 25
Mobile-Tensaw Delta, 25
Mobile Theater, 70
Montgomery, Ala., 8, 9, 10, 11, 13, 26, 66, 108
Mordecai, Solomon, 95
Morris, John, 58, 83, 113–115, 121, 124, 125
Murray, Amelia, 19, 50, 100

New Orleans, La.: climate in, 40; comparison with Mobile, 7, 119; cotton trade in, 61; health in, 74; hospitality in, 91; hotels in, 33; Lafayette's visit to, 126; Mardi Gras in, 129; newspapers in, 78; railroads near, 67; slavery in, 115–116; steamboats in, 10, 16, 17; theaters in, 121; travel to, 9; visiting, 26
New York, N.Y., 61–62
Nichols, Thomas, 104
Nott, Josiah, 97, 113

Oakleigh, 136
Oldmixon, John, 23, 40, 46, 53, 88, 90
Old Shell Road, 137
Olliffe, Charles, 59
Olmsted, Frederick Law, 30, 42, 54, 62, 86, 89–90
Outlaw Convention Center, 131

Pascagoula, Miss., 26

Pensacola, Fla., 26
Phillips, Philip, 112, 128
Phoenix Fire Museum, 137
Polk, James K., 127–128
Portier, Michael Portier, 134
Power, Tyrone, 13, 38, 47, 78
Pulszky, Francis, 19, 112, 123
Pulszky, Theresa, 19, 112, 123

Raphael Semmes House, 135
Richards, Charles G., 132
Richards-DAR House, 132
Rising Generation, 129
Roper, James, 135
Russell, Charles H., 102, 108, 109, 110
Russell, Robert, 16, 73

Samaritan Society, 73
Semmes, Raphael, 97
Sha'arai Shomayim, 94
Shakespeare's Row, 125
Shaw, John, 19, 38
Sherman, William T., 54, 97
Sledge, John, 5, 55
Smith, Sol, 121
Spring Hill College, 97, 137
Spring Hill neighborhood, 27, 73–74, 119, 137
stagecoaches, 25
steamboats, 8; description of, 10; travel hazards of, 15–16; travel on, 10, 13
Stewartfield, 137
Stockton, Ala., 16
Strikers Independent Society, 129, 130
Stuart, James, 26, 70

Tea Drinkers Society, 129
Tensaw River, 19
Thomason, Michael V. R., 5
Tombigbee River, 8, 17, 58, 66, 131
Traveller's Guide, The, 66
Turner's Society, 84

Tuscaloosa (boat), 16
Tuscaloosa, Ala., 9, 40, 66
Twelve Mile Island, 16

Union Church, 93
United States Hotel, 32

Van Buren, Martin, 126
Vassar, John Guy, 102
Vincent, Benjamin, 136
Vincent-Doan House, 136

Waverly House Hotel, 27, 29
weather, 39, 42

Welby, Victoria, 33, 87, 88, 119, 130
Whipple, Henry Benjamin, 49, 66, 90, 108, 110, 121, 125
wildlife, 35–39
Wilkinson, James, 3
William (enslaved man), 114–115
Wilson, Augusta Jane Evans, 97
Wortley, Emmeline Stuart, 54, 88, 119, 130

yellow fever, 69–73

Milton Keynes UK
Ingram Content Group UK Ltd.
UKHW041847230924
448765UK00006B/79